STARTUP ISRAEL

STARTUP ISRAEL

First Edition in 2023
Copyright © 2023 by SungAnDang

All rights reserved. No part of this publication may be reproduced, stored in a retrieval system, or transmitted, in any form or by any means, electronic, mechanical, photocopying, recording or otherwise, except as expressly permitted by law, without the prior, written permission of the publisher.

SungAnDang Publishing Company
04032 Cheomdan Building 3rd Fl., Yanghwa-ro 127, Mapo-Gu, Seoul, Republic of Korea
(TEL: 82-2-3142-0036)
10881 Moonbal-ro 112, Paju Book City, Paju, Gyeonggi-do, Republic of Korea
(TEL: 82-31-950-6300, 82-31-955-0510)
For more information, visit www.cyber.co.kr

ISBN | 978-89-315-5987-3(03320)
Price | USD 20.00

Author | David Ok
Managing Editor | Choi Ok-hyeon
Project Editor | Moon In-gon
Body Designer | Choi Yun-young, Lim Heung-soon
Cover Designer | Park Won-seok

For sales or permission outside of the Republic of Korea, please contact
Joonwon Lee(Foreign copyright manager) at jwlee@cyber.co.kr or 82-10-4624-6629

🇮🇱 **HERE COMES THAT DREAMER** 🇰🇷

STARTUP ISRAEL

DAVID OK

BM Sungandang

(THANKS TO ···)

I would like to thank my Israeli friends, Ehud Olmert, former Prime Minister of Israel, Giora Yaron, President of Tel Aviv University, Dove Moran, USB developer, Joa Gisapel, CEO of RAD Group, and Nekemia Perez, Chairman of Pithango Capital, who encouraged me, supported me, and prayed for me when I was drawing a picture on a blank sheet of paper called Israel. I would also like to thank Pastor Hwang Deok-young of Pyeongchon New Central Church, who served as a spiritual mentor, and Mayor Shin Sang-jin, who contributed to turning Pangyo into Asia's Silicon Valley. I dedicate this book to Feelux Noh Si-cheong former chairman, who served as a mentor for Korea and Israel, and my dear friend and respected CEO, the late Lim Il-taek of Kinemaster, who worked hard as KIBC CEO during the most difficult times and suddenly went to heaven."

Prologue

"Here Comes That Dreamer"

This is the first book ever that is published in my name. I have published other people's books as one of my many careers is a book publisher. At my mid age, many experiences have been accumulated. Whether I am willing or not, life goes on. I was once a young man of many visions and ambitions. I had lived my life like a courageous king. I was fearless and a man of straightforward words like a bulldozer. And Israel came to my turbulent life. I had never thought about Israel other than the birth place of Jesus and sacred land of pilgrims, a land that is enemy to 1.3 billion Middle Eastern countries.

However after watching documentary filmed by director Brad Kim, Israel became a huge part of my life. A country of small population of 9 million is leading the world, and this knowledge was shaking me to the core. After this remarkable encounter, how Israel fights Arabs who are larger than them by 15 times in population, was no longer a surprise. Israel owns most of world's wealth and its money power moves the world. Israel is the center of the world economy that molds the world. The core strength of this global influence dwells in Israel's global startup ecosystem. One man entrepreneur of a startup launches his homepage in English prior to Hebrew. Why is that so? This is because global entrepreneurship is deeply rooted in Hebrew people since the birth.

Israel's global entrepreneurship is deeply founded in courage for new things and not fearing failures. Even failures in business occur, the challenge cannot be stopped. Most Israelis believe in next opportunities. A single failure is just a stepping stone for a greater success. This outstanding courage of Israelis is not something that we commonly experience, which becomes hard to understand Israel as a nation. Therefore every time I introduce Israel, I speak of the spirit of Hutzpa.

The spirit of Hutzpa can be explained as baldness, fearlessness and faceless. But I translate in Korean as 'an iron will'. Because the spirit of Hutzpa is about not giving up and accepting new challenges. After learning about Israel, I myself have become a Hutzpa entrepreneur. Like a young man who overcomes endless challenges. This is through encounters with leading Israeli figures such as global entrepreneurs and chair of universities in forums. Israel has become the gift and blessing of my life to embrace infinite dreams, challenges and accomplishments.

After adapting the startup DNA of Israel to myself, I founded a startup company. KKUMER space in Hapjeong, Seoul to incubate young entrepreneurs. In 2010, when IT industry was booming, I started CEO MBA of young prominent entrepreneurs. I invited successful entrepreneurs to instruct seminars to share successful business tactics. This resulted in many successful enterprises such as SIWON English School, INNORED, Hello Kitty, Porridge Story, [Jeisys Medical], [KineMaster] under this mentorship. These members of Korea CEOs went to Israel to get inspirations from Israeli entrepreneurs. This group of committees is KOREA ISRAEL BUSINESS COUNCIL.

Now I have three startup incubators in Hapjeong, Pangyo and Namsan. One of Hapjeong Startup Incubators is located in a building with a scenery of 63 Building and Korea Parliament House. I believe a dreamer never gets old. Because a dreamer is actively living his dreams instead of aging. My age is nearly 60, but I still actively live my dreams. There is a famous tourist attraction, called London Eye in UK. I vision on the valley of Yanghwajin, overlooking Han river, to build Seoul Eye greater than London Eye to make it as a global landmark. To make this dream come true, I hold meetings with investors and landlords of this location.

Some who have heard of Seoul Eye plan, often ask me,
"do you have enough fund to build Seoul Eye?"
And I answer them
"Of course I don't"

Realistically speaking, in order to build Seoul Eye, it needs at least three billion KRW. But I don't do business with money. Then how am I going to execute the plan? Money does not make vision come true. Money is just a tool for vision, not the other way. A vision requires money but a vision is worth more than money.

I do not have enough money for now but I have adequate network of experts and I have an iron will and fearless spirit. There is a famous saying of the late Hyundai CEO, Jeong Ju-young which is my life's motto.

"Do it now. Do it until succeed. Do it until death"

I have never met the late CEO Jeong Ju-young. But I had had a chance to meet the daughter of the late CEO Jeong Ju-young who is Executive Director of Hyundai Asan Foundation. This encounter was through the former minister of Small and Medium Business Administration, Han Jeong-hwa when he was chairman of Hyundai Asan Foundation. At the meeting, I told to Jeong Nam-e Executive Director how his grandfather shaped my life's motto and how his entrepreneurship still wakens and inspires many entrepreneurs in Korea.

> A visionary is never afraid of the lack of money.
> A visionary is spiritually alive.
> A visionary knows no surrender.
> A visionary is not afraid of others.
> A visionary is independent.
> A visionary is overwhelmed by happiness and joy.

I call visionaries 'KKUMER'. This title is a self made term that combines a Korean word KKUM(dream) and English suffix '-er', which means 'dreamer'. I call a space of KKUMERS 'KKUMER playground'. I have three KKUMER spaces in Hapjeong, Pankyo and in Namsan.

It is largely mistaken if one assumes I have these incubator centers accomplished because of financial stability. Instead, my assets are people who validate and encourage the vision of KKUMER Space. I draw my vision on a blank canvas and people in KKUMER network invest in this illustrated vision. However I am never desperate for investment because what I need is vision not money. I like people who are likeminded.

I am a global startup founder. Firstly, collaboration of Israel and Korea and now I am looking to enlarge my territory to the great country, the US. Strong manufacture industry Korea and cutting edge technologies of global entrepreneurship of Israel will make great synergy to make it to the top. I was without fund at my initiation to reach this destination. Many mock and criticize me, saying I would not make it. However I defied all odds by taking every step one by one miraculously. Ironically these hardships only made me stronger. When I said I met the former Prime Minister of Israel and global entrepreneurs, everyone laughed at me in unbelief. But now, I have become the bridge to Israeli VIPs. How was it possible? My long friend Israeli VIPs address me;

'David, you are Israel'

The Israeli VIPs are global giants. But I persistently knocked on their seemingly unclimbable wall time after time. I invited them over to South Korea and opened business conference for four times to build a strong relation between two nations. This business conference, gathering promising entrepreneurs of both nations, easily costs more than five billion won each time. However I could not give up on my passion for Israel. As a result, I have become one of trusted bridges between entrepreneurs of Korea and Israel.

Now I am planning to launch 'Seoul Eye' in Hapjeong to resemble the unique architecture of Santorini in Greek in the heart of one of most trendy locations in Korea, called Hongdae, expecting this town to be a global startup town.

Yesterday, an acquaintance of mine came to the rooftop of KKUMER Playground overlooking Han-river, listening to my vision about SEOUL eye and said;

> "David, it seems like a plan that is going to take at least ten years..I will watch your dream"

I lived my dreams. Not because I was wealthy, able, or influential but because I had passion. When I faced obstacles, I stood up again and endured life's hardships by praying to Elohim of Israel. I do not boast my abilities but I want to witness to people around me by setting an example of how a visionary makes it to a reality. Many of young generation suffer because of the lack of vision. When the world of young men's dreams come true sets forth before our eyes, young generation no longer needs to suffer. This is the world I dream of.

> "I want to make a world, country and a nation where dreams come true"

I dream a happy dream today. Every time I struggle and want to give up, I look into my dream. A vision of a society and a country where visionaries live happily. So I hope that young generation does not give up on their visions because a man without vision is miserable.

These are words that I want to engrave to my grave

> "A man who lived his vision, I dedicate it all to young men in Korea"

Foreword

Dr. Giora Yaron (Former Chairman of Tel Aviv University)

South Korea and Israel have been sharing similar values since their inception over to 70 years ago. The countries have established relations close to 60 years ago. These relations have been accelerated with the foundation of KIBC [Korea Israel Business Forum] with Mr David Ok Chairing the Korean side and Dr. Yaron Chairing the Israeli side. The objective of the KIBC is to accelerate the collaboration between the two countries in the area of high tech: The Korean partners contribute from their knowledge of building huge conglomerates and the Israeli partners share their knowledge of what it takes to build a Start Up Nation ecosystem.

The opening of Korea-Israel Dream Center in the center of Seoul could serve as a tourist attraction that will further enhance these relation which are so important to both of our countries.

Foreword

Dov Moran (The inventor of USB)

For thousands of years, Korean and Jewish people suffered, each nation in its own way. ROK and Israel were established in the same year, 1948. From that time, each country was attacked and put into danger many times. We share many similarities. We love technology and progress. We are involved in the deep future – what will shape the human being's horizon. Israel is known for its start-up mentality. Many entrepreneurs and now many unicorns. I am so happy to see David and his book about the Israeli start-up ecosystem pushing hard for encouraging entrepreneurship in Korea. I wish David and Korea great success and I hope to see closer relations among our nations and countries.

Foreword

Jeon Ha-jin (Former CEO of Hancom Inc/Chairman of the board of SDX Foundation)

David Ok is born with Israel's DNA. With him, there is nothing impossible. He dreams and pursues his dreams with his life. He is one of few visionaries who live their visions. This does not mean that he was born privileged. He built Korea and Israel relation with his bear hands and reached the destination that he is at now After reading this book, you can understand why Israel has become the world's first from the world's best. The world is changing, and there are Jewish Americans who lead global changes. That's why I recommend this book to all businessmen who start up.

"HERE COMES THAT DREAMER."

CONTENTS

Prologue · 5

Foreword · 11

CHAPTER 01 **Israel Startup Story** · 19

History of hardship and persecution of Israel and global startup · 20

Original technologies & Patents of Israel's startup · 24

Becoming the pioneer before becoming the best · 28

Success through Failure · 33

Changing the world, instead of chasing after profit · 36

The difference between Global Startup Incubating Universities · 40

Why Korea is behind Israel · 44

Israel as the major business hub of global CEOs · 48

How Israel Innovation Authority(IIA) is leading future industry · 53

Israel's Startup Mecca, Tel Aviv University · 59

Israeli Ambassadors in South Korea · 64

Israel Project for Globlal Startup of Geyonggido · 69

CHAPTER 02 **Global Israel KKUMERS** · 75

Former Startup Israel Prime Minister, Yehud Olmert · 76

Former Chairman of Tel Aviv University, Giora Yaron · 81

CEO of Yozma Fund, Yigal Erlich · 84

CEO of RAD Group, Zohar Zisapel · 87

Father of Israel's Startup, Yossi Vardi · 91

General Secretary of Technion University, Peres Ravi · 96

President of Startup VC Pitango, Nechemia Peres · 103

CEO of Audiocodes, Shabtai Adlersberg · 111

Vice President of Weizmann Lab, Dr. Mudi Sheves · 116

Nobel Prize Winner, Professor Robert Aumann · 122

Vice President of Check Point, Dorit Dor · 128

CHAPTER 03 **KKUMER story** · 133

KKUMER questions · 134

KKUMER acts · 138

KKUMER pays the price · 141

KKUMER grows through failures · 145

KKUMER fixes kennel twelve times · 149

KKUMER rises from despair · 152

KKUMER leads the future · 158

Investing in Global Entrepreneurs and Enterprises · 161

The London Eye of Seoul in Hapjeong · 168

The next Korea's Israeli Ambassador · 175

KKUMER Playground is a Vision Stage for the Next Generation · 182

CHAPTER 04 **Technologies that Change the World** · 203

Self Driving Car is the Key to Future · 204

Self Driving Car is the Major Future Industry of Korea · 209

Cyber Security is the Core Technology of Self Driving Car · 212

Metaverse; Worldview and Storytelling beyond Technology · 216

CHAPTER 01

Israel Startup Story

History of hardship and persecution of Israel and global startup

Israel has only one tenth population and land of South Korea. However a small country like Israel dominates world economy and power. What would it mean to South Koreans? It teaches us how a small country can survive in global competence; a country that has similar history and tradition to South Korea, is a leading nation of world's powerful countries.

Where does the power of Israel come from? It is from globalization. The power of Israel starts from global culture. Israelis are fluent in English

▲ Yoon Jong-rok, former Vice Minister of Science, ICT and Future Planning, Ehud Olmert, former Israeli Prime Minister, Noh Si-cheong, former Chairman of Feelux, and Robert Aumann, Hebrew University professor (from left to right) at the Korea-Israel Business Forum.

and in their third language of choice. They were diasporas throughout the world 2,000 years and learned to survive in different cultures and countries.

Everywhere you go, there is vigilance against foreigners. There are different regulations and cultures from small town to another. A foreign country has its own historical and cultural customs and cultures different to one's hometown. From early on, Israelis have been constantly the target to the surrounding Arabian countries. Israel also has its own dark history of being colonized by other countries.

On the other hand, Israel also has golden age where Arabian countries had to pay homage to Israel. However in the middle age, Israel was struck down by the strongest empire of the time, Rome and it was colonized once again. At that time, Rome was afraid of colonizing Israel, foreseeing that it would lead to a big revolt for independence. So Rome decided to scatter them instead.

And Rome moved Palestines to where Israelis originally lived so that the land of Israel could be permanently removed. After 2,000 years had gone by, the nation of Israel was born in the land of Israel. During two millenniums, Israel was wandering around the world.

Although Israelites were without a home land but its ethnicity was never lost. They didn't forget Hebrews but also adopted foreign languages and became globalized. Nation of Israel is established from overcoming hardship and they gained money power.

Wherever Israelis go, they occupy the best landmark. Israelites prefer cash and do not put credit in invisible assets. 90% of diamond industry is owned by Jews. Jews could not stay in one area for too long due to persecution.

Due to the harsh persecution towards people of Israel, Jews pioneered in jewelry and finance businesses. However when the riches of Jews spread through the word of mouth, many robbers tried to steal their fortune. To avoid the constant threats, Jews founded credit card system to carry cash in handy. In the same manner, Jews dominated jewelry industry to carry large fortune in one dime.

Therefore the utmost priority for Jews was survival and this transformed their businesses to be mobile and exchangeable to cash at all times. The M&A industry was also pioneered by Israelites. All these successful outcomes were shaped by a long history of hardship and persecution that Israelis endured for thousands of years.

In WWII, approximately six million European Jews were massacred. They were massacred without knowing the reason but suffered immeasurable pain and persecution. The survivors also suffered inhumane tortures such as being dumped in the toilet and hung by electronic cords.

Korea also was colonized under Japan for 35 years. Like Jews, Koreans underwent painful suffering and persecution. However the difference between Korea and Israel is that Korea had not had a closure with Japan in many historical conflicts. There is a famous saying by Jews when German kneeled down to seek forgiveness

"Forgive but never forget"

Yes, Indeed. Israel's global startup started with long suffering and persecution. However these hardships blossomed into a fervent soil for Israel to prosper. The world is ruled by Jews. Economy, culture, education, energy and all industries have been conquered by Jews. They resolved their long painful history by global startup.

The only key for Korea to succeed in a global market is to benchmark Israel. Learning from their history and adopting into Korea's own strategies will lead South Korea into one of the strongest countries. I believe more Koreans need to visit Israel to learn global startup culture. Korean government should encourage to send more students to Israel. When Hutzpa spirit meets Korea's iron will, Korea can lead global economy.

Original technologies
& Patents of Israel's startup

The core values of Israel's startup are globalization and technology. Israel had already experienced globalization very early on. Because Israel lived scattered all around the world for 2,000 years and they had to find ways to survive in various foreign regions. I was shocked to find a Jewish ghetto even in a rural area where Uyghur tribe lives in China.

As means of survival, they invented technologies. Every profitable industry is dominated by Jews. They prefer those who hunt their own eatery rather than those who purchase food. Those who purchase food earn money but those who hunt their own eatery, can survive through their hunting skills.

▲ Dr. Mudi Sheves, Vice President, welcoming attendees at the 1st KIBF held at the Weizmann Institute of Science.

The excellence of Jews is that they don't just adopt technologies but invent original technologies and develop into core technologies that are highly profitable. When Jews invest in a product, it becomes commercially successful and dominates industry.

The most influential figures in the world's leadership are Jews and I have tapped into a powerful network of Jews and become friends with them. This network taught me why Jews excel in what they do.

In Israel, there is Weizmann Institute of Science, which is one of the world's top five science institutions. Weizmann is a global science institution that consists of influential figures such as Max Karl Ernst Ludwig Planck, a German theoretical physicist and Louis Pasteur, a French biochemistry. It has come two Nobel prize winners and two Israeli prime ministers in succession. It was named after one of early prime ministers of Israel, Chaim Weizmann.

▲ Portrait of Dr. Chaim Weizmann, the first President of Israel who founded the Weizmann Institute of Science.

This is where I visit when I make a yearly trip to Israel with Korea's VIPs. At this place, average 1,000 patents and intellectual properties are commercialized and made profitable by technology transfer every year. This is why Weizmann has its own independent enterprise YEDA that specializes in technology transfer of intellectual properties.

There are several companies that made huge profit from YEDA. One of them is German's multinational pharmaceutical company, MERCK. They transferred core technology of multiple sclerosis cure that decreases symptoms by more than 30% and commercialized the cure that made 1.8 billion Euro.

CEO of YEDA, the technology transfer specialized enterprise is Doctor Mordechai Shevez. He has a tender appearance with a generous heart. I have known him for seven years. He always provides a personal guide to Weizmann Institute of Science and takes special care for Korean visitors.

▲ Korean CEOs visiting the Weizmann Institute of Science are listening to explanations from employees.

Why is he so kind to us? Of course, friendship is important but business is business. He is my business partner in which I bridge Korea's pharmaceutical companies to transfer technologies from YEDA. He is the key figure to access YEDA's technology transfers.

YEDA of Weizmann Institute of Science, has 28 billion dollars of sales so far. Every year they earn more than [100 billion] for loyalty only. Weizmann Institute of Science is an academic science institution as well as a large business enterprise. Which company in Korea can turn their scientific findings to a successful business model?

How do researchers of Weizmann Institute of Science make such remarkable outcomes? Firstly, they are free from the burden of responsibilities with success of their research outcomes but they are constantly encouraged to literately continue in their investigations as long as they want until the next investigator takes a turn.

Secondly, researchers occupy 40% of profit when their technologies get transferred and Weizmann owns 60%. This profit share system enriches researchers of Weizmann.

I hope that South Korea will come forth a global science research institution like Weizmann. An institution that does not rely on government fund but is financially independent like YEDA of Weizmann. The fair distribute of profit according to each researcher's contribution will make the business self sustainable.

Becoming the pioneer before becoming the best

New industries of the world are now dominated by those who develop technologies and commercialize them. For a product to enter a market after a successful collaboration of various technologies, undergoes many obstacles. This issue exists in every country all around the world.

There is a Korean company that pioneers blood glucose measurement industry. Conventional way to measure blood glucose is by extracting blood. This method is employed by almost all blood glucose measuring devices. For example, you have to poke the tip of a finger to measure blood glucose. Diabetes patients have to measure blood glucose everyday to treat the

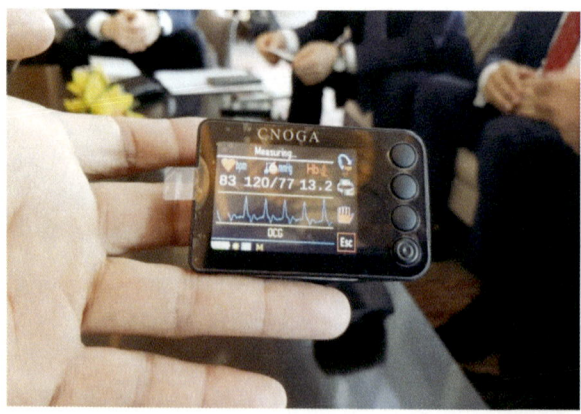

▲ World's first non-invasive blood glucose meter.

condition.

Imagine. How painful would it be to extract blood from the tip of a finger every single day? It is a burdensome and painful task. I, myself, have diabetes so it is one of my daily tasks in order to prevent complications.

However, I cannot carry on this painful daily task of blood glucose measurement because it's simply too painful and troublesome for a everyday task. Firstly, I do not like the feeling of pain. Secondly, it is too tiresome to do it on a daily base.

Can there be way to measure blood sugar level without extracting blood? Until now, blood is the most accurate way to measure many diseases such as high blood pressure and diabetes. But is there any other way than this painful and tiresome method of blood extraction? Beginning of a new business is recognizing inconvenience of customers and providing a solution. In South Korea, we have people who are trying to find new ways to measure diseases such as high blood pressure and diabetes without blood extraction.

However there has not been successful cases just yet. Usually people compete with existing advanced technologies rather than inventing new technologies to pioneer a new market. South Korea had been under continuous invasion by other strong countries for 500 years in Choseon dynasty. As a result people in South Korea long for a stable lifestyle rather than taking challenges and risks.

On the other hand, Israel lived without homeland scattered all over the world for two millennial. Ethnicity exists but nation of Israel didn't exist. So they were refugees wandering around the world. Their diaspora journey took 2,000 years. There is a Korean saying which goes 'suffering starts after leaving home door'. How about Israel? A nation survived without homeland.

For Jews, business is a matter of survivor. They did business as a survival matter everywhere they went. They did not do it easy way. They had to sustain their lives in foreign countries where they were not welcome. This is why Jews became experts in business, recognizing people's needs and solving them with their inventive technologies.

Jews make money by analyzing consumer pattern and demands and accurately solving it. They analyze data to find out consumer demands and develop a scenario to execute it realistically. This area of consumer analysis is what they excel in and this is why they develop new technologies rather than being the best in already existing technologies.

Generally, blood glucose measuring devices use blood extraction. However Israel's startup invented blood glucose measuring device without blood extraction. Then what happened to Korea's researchers for blood glucose measuring device without blood extraction? They also were supported by Korea's government. However why didn't Korea's investigators succeed in their development?

There are various reasons. Firstly, they do not have sufficient scientific knowledge. Secondly, Korea's science infrastructure is poor. Thirdly, the lack of persistency is another reason. Israelis engineers press on their given tasks even if they fail. How do Israelis persistently investigate and commercialize their R&D projects?

In Israel, there is a global science institution, Weizmann. In Weizmann, there are 200 global scientists. When a task is given, investigators investigate until their investigations are complete and they present the outcome. If someone who is in the process of investigation passes away, another investigator comes along and completes the task. They have a full system and drive to complete their investigation. This is not done over night.

To be the best in the world, you have to develop original technology. In

▲ Together with Alon Kapel, the Asia Director of Cnoga, which developed the world's first non-invasive blood glucose meter.

order to do so, Korea has to shift paradigm. Everyone wants stability in their life but compromises cannot reach the top. Someone who pioneers without compromising for stable life will become the best. This is the privilege entitled to pioneers.

I am hoping that Korea will focus on founding original technology. If one becomes pioneer, he can be the best. Cnoga, that invented non-invasive glucometer was invested 50 billion won by Chinese global company, BOE group. This made Cgona a global enterprise. Cnoga persisted on developing non-invasive glucometer from the beginning without compromises despite of many challenges.

The success didn't come at first for Cnoga. It took numerous painful failures. A path that has been walked before is an easy path. Anyone can walk there. However a path that has never been walked before is a challenging path. Solitude and despairs come. However persisting without ceasing will eventually pay its prize.

A well made product does not need extra marketing nor exclusive distribution channels. Because, original technology already has high scarcity that makes it the best. However developing original technology takes enormous amount of efforts to execute it. I believe Korean engineers can invent original technologies.

Success through Failure

The busiest man in the world… Dov Moran, the inventor of USB is the most intriguing man since I have entered the world of Israel. As USB is one of the most innovative inventions in the world, I had much questions before meeting with him. What is in his mind? What kind of attitude does he have for his life?

With many questions queuing in my mind, I went to meet him. The most surprising thing about Mr.Moran was that he was an ordinary and modest man. When meeting famous people in Korea, they have some type of bluff. I have never experienced anyone influential in Korea to be down

▲ Together at Dov Moran's Comigo headquarters.

to earth. Why is that so? This is because Korea had undergone rapid generational changes that lack value and philosophy.

I was surprised by his honest and humorous tone and manner in his tieless shirt attire. He asked me;

> "How many times have you failed?"

This was the first question he had for me. I answered with smiling;

> "Too many, I lost the track of counting"

Since then, he treated me like a friend. Now we contact each other like a long term friend. Every time I hold a meeting with business CEOs and university professionals, I ask them the same question.

> "How many times have you failed?"

If the person cannot answer frankly, I have difficulties in pursuing the conversation further. Dov is a famous CEO because everyone has USB. After inventing USB, he succeeded in M&A with Sandisk Global for 1.7 trillion won. This is a remarkable record breaking deal for an individual's invention to close a deal worth more than 1 trillion won with America's global company. From this deal, he quickly became a world-famous CEO.

However he started failing ever since. He earned enormous amount of money. What would an ordinary Korean business man do? He would buy a building then he would invest in real estates and financial products to build evenly distributed portfolio of his wealth. This is the difference between entrepreneurship of Korea and Israel.

After selling USB, he continued investing in startups. He still invests in many startups. The greatness of Moran is that after enormous success of USB, he still is not afraid of failures in taking new challenges. He once said in his TV interview.

> "I want my bank account to be zero when I die. I want to keep investing in startups to pass on entrepreneurship as a legacy to next generation"

Every time I visit Israel or he visits Korea, we always hold a meeting. He still says this every time we meet. "Are you failing? Then that means you live well. The biggest slump could be when people think they are well-off"

In November 2016, Korean university professors and I made a visit to Dov Moran's office. And he popped the same question to them.

> "How many times have you failed?"

Every time I feel exhausted and want to give up, I think of him. He is an icon of failure and success. Moran says you can only succeed after you fail and his insightful words really encourage me. I am hoping that our nation would have entrepreneurs like Dov Moran.

Changing the world, instead of chasing after profit

What is the most significant thing in life? Many people have unclear goals in their lives. In other words, they live as life takes them. I don't have an intention of criticizing lifestyles of others. Because there are different lifestyles and life goals for each one.

There is a Korean idiom;

"Tigers leaves leather when it dies but a man leaves his name when he dies"

Life leaves its traces. It means everyone draws different life pictures. What is the purpose of earning money? Ultimately, people want a happy life to enjoy.

But does making a large sum of money make a person happy? Wealth makes life convenient. However money cannot buy you happiness. Convenience does not necessarily guarantee happiness in life. However people like to own fortune as a means of happiness.

Nation of Israel spent 2,000 years without a homeland. This made Jews desperate for money. Because money secures their lives in foreign countries hence Jews are skillful in making money better than any other nation.

However there is one thing that Jews ought to do once they get rich. They spent their fortune for the benefit of the nation and furthermore for the world. Jews donate generous amount of money to form communities. And these donations are used to change the world. What does it mean by changing the world? It means making the world a better place.

Technologies in this world continues to advance. In this highly industrialized world, everything is now becoming digitalized. One must study the shift social changes in order to adapt to a new lifestyle. Previous generations who are not as skillful with computers as present generation are likely to have an unclear future. One must study to adapt the coming digital era otherwise they will be ultimately left behind.

However if technologies are invented to be easily adapted by elder generation, it will solve much inconvenience. Advancement of technologies are to make the world more convenient and better. Despite of gender and age, it is convenience of technologies that will become part of daily lives at the end of the day.

The core value of Israeli startup is original technology. It is advancement in manufacture, service, IT technology that will better the world more than platform and community. Therefore Israel startups have paved new paths that no one ever paved before such as auto-mobility.

The most important thing about auto-mobility is to develop a technology that acts as human eyes. A technology that performs as good as human sight is a highly advanced technology. Human's eye is created by a creator. Can technology mimic the creation? However artificial technology is almost catching up with divine work.

There is an Israeli startup that developed artificial eye successfully. It's called 'Mobile Eye' founded by professor of Hebrew University, Shashua Amnon. This startup was sold to Intel by 17.56 trillion won in 2017. This is by far one of the most astronomically large scale of M&A with tremendous amount of money.

People discuss price for M&A. But Israelis weighs more on value that a technology will create for human kind. Yes. Technologies brings money but this is rather an instant success. Earning money and spending money is two different things.

Israel Startup is not only about making large fortune, but to make the world better. When While Korea's successful business man invests in real estates, Israeli entrepreneurs invest in becoming a serial entrepreneur.

Even though I made a good fortune through IT, I try to make a new business model to help and encourage the next generation. In Israel, a person does not change his lifestyle after making a large fortune. Because his values and beliefs do not change.

It is not money that changes the world. It's a technology that changes the world. Therefore advancement of technology is same as changing the world. Changing the world means to improve qualities of life and promotes happiness through technologies. Therefore what's more important than making money is to build a future society through reliable technologies.

The world ought to innovate technologies. The better world with improved convenience is achieved through technology inventions. Therefore Israel startup is global, future forward and humane for a better creation world. We, Koreans should challenge ourselves to innovate technologies to better the world.

The difference
between Global Startup Incubating Universities

In November 2016, I was on the way to Israel in an airplane. This trip was for MOU between Israeli Universities and Korean Universities and for Korean professors to experience Israeli Startup Leadership in the field. Please understand that I will be using initials instead of real names for confidentiality. Because Korea has just stepped its very first step in global startup ecosystem.

The purpose for going to universities is clear in Israel. In Israel, people only

▲ Signing ceremony of MOU between Tel Aviv University's Faculty of Engineering (Dean Rosenwaks) and Ewha Womans University in Korea.

go to university only if they have a clear purpose unlike Korea where high school graduates mandatorily enter universities. Therefore average age for 1st grade university student in Israel is 23 because Israelis go to army first before university. Army in Israel is more severe that Korean military as they fight for their survival in a real-time war.

They go to army under threats of terrorism by 1.3 billion Arabian nations. Therefore Israel army has a strong bond. Global entrepreneurship also starts in Israeli military as the strong bond built by surviving terror together in army continues in startup business.

Life driven by a clear purpose can also fail but it knows no giving up. Even though life can fail more than once it is considered hardship, but not despair. They already fought for their lives in military therefore they know how valuable and important life is before learning entrepreneurship. Israeli young generation with clear purposes go to universities after military service and their university studies excel for the sense of clear vision and purpose for their lives.

For Israel, universities are a stepping stone for startups. The biggest startup accelerator in Tel Aviv is StarTau of Tel Aviv University. In StarTau, global startup of Israel is born. The biggest asset of Israeli startups is original technology as mentioned before. This makes Israelis startups successful despite of many failures. Because their technology is one and only in the world, it has more possibility to succeed after development.

Recently, there was global top M&A endorsement. The global multinational company, Intel endorsed M&A with an enterprise with only 130 billion sales. Intel previously invested in 17.56 trillion for Israeli startup Mobil Eye. Usually such large amount of investment is spent for M&A with global top-tier companies. But the CEO of Mobil Eye is computer professor, Amnon Shashua of Hebrew University.

Global universities of Israel such as Hebrew University, Tel Aviv University, Technion University are the fervent soil for global startups. The startup infrastructure of these universities are not funded by government unlike Korea. Universities have their own R&D labs to create their own outcomes to turn highly potential inventions into intellectual properties or highly profitable business by collaborating with relevant companies.

YISUM of Hebrew University, ROMOT of Tel Aviv University, T3 Lab of Technion University are the three major R&D research labs that have made billions for their own universities. Those who gained great success through M&A then donate their earnings back to their own universities. Israeli Universities have come forth many successful entrepreneurs and these entrepreneurs give back to their universities for the support that received, with large sums of donations to be used as scholarship for the next generation.

For Korean universities, they have just taken the very first step in global startup incubation. There are 37 universities supported by government for less than a decade in Korea. For this reason, I introduce Israeli global startup ecosystem set by universities to Korean university committees. Korea still has a far way to go. There's not been enough time for Korean universities to invent original technologies as to benchmark Israeli startup ecosystem.

However Korean universities are making speedy progresses. Especially, A university has a great potential. However many universities are too burdened by the pressure to present instant outcomes. Even though there has been MOU endorsed between Korean and Israeli universities, Korea cannot learn Israeli university's global startup ecosystem without true relationship and collaboration.

I suggest to Korean universities to form a R&D team with Israeli universities for founding a startup. One needs to experience in mainstream field to learn the real world of startup. One cannot deny that the world is dominated by Jews. One needs to be part of Israeli network who have the global top network. Thankfully, the key person of Jewish VIP network is my best friend.

I hope that one day, collaboration between Korea and Israel universities R&D team will cofound a global startup in Silicon valley. I want to do my best for that day. Through my Jewish network, I want to show a new path of hope to Korean young generations and universities. With this hope in my mind, I work for Korea-Israel relation.

Why Korea is behind Israel

The disaster of Korea's economy started from building multinational companies. Korea is nicknamed 'republic of Samsung' as the country relies too much on Samsung for its economic strength. In another words, Korea will lose its economic power if Samsung sinks. Just like Finnish economy was swayed after Nokia went bankrupt.

For this reason, I have spoken my belief that Korea needs a second Samsung. This does not mean building another multinational company but rather a small yet powerful global giant company that has its roots in a lean startup system. Because it is impossible to grow another Samsung. To grown another company like Samsung, it needs generational efforts in a global environment backed up by excellent skills, which is not easy.

Moreover, it is extremely challenging to build a global distribution channel and A/S network. Quality consistency of global distribution channel and A/S network throughout the world, requires another astronomical cost. And even with the cost paid, it is another task to achieve the current global competence.

This is why Israel does not invest in huge conglomerates. From manufacture to IT industry, Israel does not invest in growing a multinational company.

This is because they are well aware of the fact that even with the enough money to fund conglomerates, it is extremely hard to accomplish a successful manufacture-based multinational company worldwide. Thus they rather invest in lean global startups.

Now, Israel has earned astronomical amount of profits off of global startups. One global startup can earn tremendous amount of money. The strength about Israeli global startup is that it becomes a large business when it makes an exit. This leads to large enough earnings to buy a huge conglomerate like Samsung electronics.

For example, the number one hot issue of global business transaction was global M&A of Mobil Eye and Intel in 2017. A small startup of Israel, Mobil Eye sold the artificial eye to Intel for 17.56 trillion. This was by far the biggest M&A sales in the history of global startup M&A. This is why Israel's startup is different from Korean startup. However there is a secret to Israel's great success in global M&A deal that one should never overlook. I summarized their strategies in three milestones.

1. Israelis startups make English homepage foremost
2. Israelis found a startup only with original technology
3. Israelis found a startup after investment attraction

What would be the reactions of Korean founders if I explain the above three strategies? Are there any Korean startup founders who would found their startup in Israel's way? Every time I encounter government officials or policy makers of Korea's startup ecosystem, I present Israeli startup ecosystem. If Korea does not design startup infrastructure as Israel's, Korea will fail.

What should then senior business men do? They should contribute to building global startup infrastructure for young generation of Korea. We should make the startup ecosystem as fervent as Israel in order for Koreans to come up with a world's renowned startup like Mobil Eye. My concern is to find senior entrepreneurs who are able to build such startup ecosystem in order to give hopes to young generation.

However this is not an overnight task. I am now in my mid 50s. Korea cannot expect to build global startup infrastructure in a short time as similar to Israel's hard earned global startup ecosystem as a result of thousand years of nation's endeavor. However I still want to make my efforts to make Korean young generation to have a vision. I know how smart and creative

▲ Intel, Mobileye, and BMW are collaborating on the development of autonomous vehicles (source: Christof Stache/AFP/Getty Images).

Korean youngsters are.

I want to dress up Korean youngsters a global attire. I want to inherit a world where people can dream together and share happiness. The one way to do that is through global startup. How wonderful would it be for Korean youngsters to learn Israelis startup model? This makes me progress my global movement daily.

Israel as the major business hub of global CEOs

The world is facing bullet-less war of economy. There could become a world where only companies at a multinational level, survive beyond government rule. Because the whole world is confronted with financial burden. The industrial revolution brought to digitalization and is now leading to the 4th industrial revolution. The question is "how would you survive in a global economic war?"

Many global companies go bankrupt overnight. Those giant companies face survival issues. In nature, dinosaurs die first before little birds when there is a food shortage. Birds need only little food but dinosaurs need a lot of food.

▲ Alibaba founder Jack Ma is receiving an honorary doctorate degree from Tel Aviv University.

Just like that, when there is economic recession, bigger companies suffer greater for survival more than small companies.

The world is reset by G2. US and China are fighting the bullet-less economic war. US has the world power and China has US national debts and dollars. It seems like they are fighting on the surface but the US is already the winner in this game. Ultimately, China has more to loose than the US. As prophesied by Dèng Xiǎopíng at his last breath, China must not revolt against the US until 2025 otherwise they will regret the consequences.

However there is a hidden winner in this world war, that is not the US nor China but Israel. Because the US is literally dominated by Israel. The Jewish Americans have the real power in the US. The former US president, Trump was born in New York, the Jewish district of America and he is a Jew to the bones. This has made the Trump administration pro-Semitism politics.

China is still a foreigner to Israel. For Chinese people to cross the Israeli border, they have to undergo a strict visa assessment. These two countries still are distant. However from 5 years ago, Chinese people were frequently spotted in Tel Aviv. I also could spot some Chinese people in Tel Aviv in my last trip to Israel for the last three years.

At first, I thought they were tourists. However I could sight these Chinese visitors at my business meetings with Israeli VIPs. Sometimes I had important meetings with Chinese global CEOs in Israel. At first, I was surprised by their visit in Tel Aviv, Israel. However as time goes by, I found out Chinese global CEOs come to Israel with clear goals.

There was a conferment ceremony held in Tel Aviv University with Jack Ma Yun of Alibaba, China. Tel Aviv University of Israel is a global academic institution. They have many graduates who are now global CEOs. They are now interested in Chinese global CEOs, calling Chinese global CEOs to come to Tel Aviv University to form an innovative group.

I have a close relationship with Chair and Vice President of TAU. Glora Yaron, who is chair of TAU is also a chairman of KIBC. Every time I make a visit to Israel, President Yaron advises Korean visitors to pay attention to Israel. Because the global CEOs of China are already forming intimate business relation with Israel, forming network as colleagues of TAU.

Chinese giant companies such as Alibaba, 10cent and BIDU are already investing large sum of money in Tel Aviv, especially in areas of medicine, medical, IT. They are buying Israel startups that have outstanding technologies. They are collecting Israeli startups that developed market approved technologies.

Why do Chinese millionaires make large investment in Israel? Why do they invest in the original technologies of Israel? Because they are aware of the fact that the future of China is at the hands of Israel. What would it mean to us? Before it's too late, Korea needs to step in the global scene with Israel.

And we need to send bright minds of Korea to Israel to learn their education and culture. After Korean War, Korea overcame its poverty by sending bright minds to the US for scholarship and when they came back to Korea, they contributed to Korea's government and companies. I believe more bright minds in Korea should go to Israel to learn their global leadership in the world economy.

There are too many pros in Israeli global startup network to ignore. We are to admit the fact that global language and culture play an advantageous role in global network to grow world leaders. Before Chinese CEOs partner with Israel, Korea needs to form an economic community with Israel.

Time is running out. If we are late, it might become too late for Israelis to open business opportunities for Korea. Jews are practical and money-wise. If Korea does not provide what Israel needs, China will penetrate between Korea and Israel's relation and will become the key country of Asia. This is not my opinion. This is the message that Chinese CEOs are persuading Israel with.

Why CEOs of Alibaba, 10cent and BIDU are eager to invest in Israel and cofound a company with Israel? Alibaba is already aware of Israel's worth in terms of human resource and technology that makes investment worthwhile. 10cent already made large sum of investment in smart farm. BIDU invested in artificial eye of Mobil Eye and auto-mobility.

Innovation is not for everyone. It takes guts to overcome constant criticism. Many youngsters are looking for stability and prosperity in their lives so they seek for jobs as government officers or employees in big companies. I want to let Korean youngsters to know why Chinese CEOs invest in Israel and how Korean government needs to invest in Israel to secure future industries. However my message to wake the people of Korea does not get crossed easily. I hope my concerns for the nation of Korea will bring a positive reality soon.

How Israel Innovation Authority(IIA) is leading future industry

Israel is full of amazement; the more you delve into, the more treasures you will find. A small nation of 9 million population has world's leading technologies and cultural heritages, overcoming constant pressure and threat from 1.3 billion Arabians.

Israel as a nation has a top priority. It is to create a prosperous future industry for the nation and provides support for it. Since 1969, Israel established Office of Chief Scientists, an institution that determines economic policies based on technology development.

The Prime Minister of Israel registered many technology and economic policies for agriculture and defense of Israel for its global growth. It's called OCS (Office of Chief Scientist). It's a unique system, mixing government and civil institutions.

It is funded by government however it's operated by a civil organization. Employees are government officials but the institution is operated at a civil level. How unusual is it? What does it mean by 'government funded to be operated by civil'?

This is a business model that only exists in Israel. What does the workplace of collaboration of government officials and civil worker mean? How is this model even possible? Only Israel can make it work. When government organization is run by civil workers, it creates effective outcomes from a healthy tension that exists between government and civilians.

OCS was established in 1969 and it went through another innovation in 2016. It was used to be called OCS but it was later innovated with a new name, IIA (Israel Innovation Authority), to be more specific in its specialty in creating future industries.

Ultimately, in order to add innovation and liberation to OCS of Israel, it was transformed to IIA. Its head person is the best expert in the profession. The CEO of IIA (Israel Innovation Authority) is the best expert in the his expertise.

CEO of IIA is Dror Bin and Amiram Applebaum is Chairman. Amiram Applebaum is the former CEO of KLA Tencer, that had one of the best technologies in Silicon Valley. KLA Tencer has market capitalization of 56 billion in semiconductor industry. Hiring the best expert in the civil area as CEO of IIA is an exceptional strategy of Israel.

President of IIA is Dror Bin of RAD Group who has built the world's best telecommunication technology. RAD Group is not widely known in South Korea however it is Israel's IT innovation company that listed 3 companies to NASDAQ.

IIA hired one of the best experts from civli global groups of Silicon Valley as CEO and President, to create synergy from collaboration of government officials and civil entrepreneurs to execute the best performance. This is an exceptional insight of Israel to create promising future industry.

There are 6 departments of IIA.

1. Department of Innovation ; incubating original technology base entrepreneurs
2. Department of R&D ; Scale-up entrepreneurs
3. Department of Infrastructure Development for Technology Innovation
4. Department of Environment and Attracting businesses for global collaboration
5. Department of Various Support and Program Development for Manufacture Innovation
6. Department of Policy Making and Business Promotion for Regional Innovative Environment Development

IIA is the world's first global innovation organization that transferred all responsibilities and authorities to civil leadership. This is only model that exists in Israel where collaboration between government officials and civil workers exist.

In 2022, the business model of IIA does not stay in the present reality. They are discussing policies and technology development for the future of Israel in 30 years time. Even it doesn't bring immediate profits, they invest

500 billion annually for making effective future policies and technology development.

In South Korea, we have a similar organization. Under former president of South Korea, Park Chung-hee, there was an organization for economic development in 5 years and this contributed to the growth of shipbuilding, semiconductor, and manufacturing. The current economic wealth of South Korea was because of the implementation of his plan.

What is the future industry for South Korea? What can we do to prepare future? What would be South Korea's major industry? The dictatorship of Park Chung-hee administration is criticized for anti demographic nature however one cannot deny his contribution to the preparedness for the future economic strength of South Korea.

What is happening to the future of South Korea? The brightest minds of South Korea must gather to prepare future industry. For this purpose, I had a meeting with CEOs of IIA and studied their system.

I dare to dream to build Korea's Innovation Authority after IIA's model. I am not a president of South Korea, but if I were, I would build Korea's Innovation Authority foremost so that Korea can be a member of G7 in 30 years time. There are many bright minds in the world but not everyone can execute their plan to reality.

A leader is to position human resource in the right time and place and develop policies to generate highest synergy and effectiveness. A president and general of a country are positions that consider for the future industry of a country and develop and legitimate proper policies to execute them.

South Korea is ought to have its own Innovation Authority institution to prepare for the coming 30 years. What would it be like for the next generation when they cannot fsee a promising future? The world is at war of economy without bullets. A murder can easily happen without bullets.

How should we be welcoming the future? If we don't prepare for the future, our offsprings will suffer its consequences. What legacy can we leave to our offsprings? If we don't think now, they will inherit poverty as our previous generation suffered.

Future belongs to those who prepare. How can we prepare our future? What can we do as seniors to inherit a proud future for the next generation? We are to give up on personal greeds to prepare otherwise national disasters will overwhelm us.

This disaster is not a catastrophic disaster but it will be an economic disaster as a result of the lack of global competence. South America used to be wealthier than South Korea. They had rich underground resources that made them one of the most powerful countries of the world.

Unfortunately, South American fell because they didn't prepare for the future. The stage of future should be built by a country. In another words, a nation should lead with directions because individual's efforts are risky and time-consuming. What would you do? What would Korea as a nation do for the better future? If we don't take that into consideration now, we will fall like South America.

What are you going to inherit to the next generation? This is the task that adults should solve, society should hold responsibility for and a nation to take as an obligation. If a nation does not take the future industry into serious considerations, our offsprings will inherit nothing but poverty.

"What kind of world are you going to inherit to your child?"

Israel's Startup Mecca, Tel Aviv University

What is one of the first things that comes to your mind when you hear about Israel? It's Jerusalem. One of the first impressions about Israel is Jerusalem as it is the symbol of Israel. But how about when we ask world economic leaders the same question? They would response it to be 'Tel Aviv'.

Jerusalem is a city of religion. For this reason, many think many qualities of Israel to be equivalent to what Jerusalem represents. At first, I also thought of Jerusalem first when I thought about Israel. This was why I opened the first Korea Israel Business Forum at Jerusalem. However after staying in Tel Aviv for three days after the forum, I realized my choice of venue was wrong.

Jerusalem is the capital of Israel and Tel Aviv is economic capital of Israel. Tel Aviv has a scenery similar to many European vacation sites. There are world's top-tiered hotels along side of the seashore of Tel Aviv, overlooking endless horizon of the ocean. I stayed in Renaissance Hotel by Tel Aviv beach, reviewing my thoughts about Israel and being inspired with new ideas.

Tel Aviv is just like Silicon Valley. Many multinational companies initiated as Israeli startups could be easily spotted in Tel Aviv such as WIX.COM and Waze Mobile, which was sold to Google for 1.6 trillion won. The heart of Israeli Startup is at Tel Aviv.

One of the most important startup incubation center is Tel Aviv University owned institution, called STARTAU. STARTAU has its unique business model. Share holders of STARTAU are student union by 10%, TAU by 10% and the rest of 80% share is owned by business enterprises that support STARTAU. STARTAU's share holder system creates exceptional and liberating dynamics of STARTAU.

The year I met Joseph Klafter, the eighth President of TAU was in Autumn in the year of 2012. It was when founders of Korea Venture Business Association were invited by TAU. Joseph Klafter fondly gave a speech about TAU. I was amazed by his kind and personal approach.

I did not expect a president of global university such TAU would welcome us in such a personal manner. I have only one close relationship with one chairman of Korea's university. I do not have network with any VIPs of Seoul University, Yonsei University or Korea University. To be honest, I do not want to get to know them. It takes painstakingly long time and large amount of efforts to get to know them.

Ironically, with Israel, I have a connection with Joseph Klafter of TAU. In his office and personal space, I freely have conversations about intellectual exchanges between universities of Korea and Israel to drive MOU between government departments of both countries. What is global? It's simple. If one knows Jewish network, it's global. Who dominates the world? It's Jews.

The formation of network between Korea and Israel for the mutual development has been mostly contributed by TAU. For a mutual communication, both parties have to be at the same level. In another words, there needs to be a direct communication between two universities such as co-R&D investigations and exchange student programs.

However Korea's government and universities tend to stay on a surface level when it comes to global collaboration. For example, if there is a successful MOU between governments and universities between two nations, there needs to be post maintenance management such as promoting exchange student programs. Especially, affiliating with startup leading universities such as TAU, there needs to be co-startup achievements from this affiliate. Although Israel is ready, Korea is not as ready.

It is embarrassing to admit that the reason for this delay of post maintenance management of the affiliate, is the lack of Korea's capacity for this partnership. Israel is the top tier country in the world but Korea is not as advanced. There is a gap. How do we make it possible for Korea to take a leap over its obstacles? Korea needs to visit Israel to learn. Then what is the best method to learn Israeli startup?

I believe 30 brightest minds in Korean young generation needs to take abroad inspection to learn in STARTAU. And then they need to form a dream team with Israelis. We want to enlarge our territory to Silicon Valley but Silicon Valley does not favor Korea.

▲ Together with Joseph Klafter, the President of Tel Aviv University, at his office.

The only nation Silicon Valley is fond of is Israel. Silicon Valley is ruled by Jewish mafia. This is why we need to learn Israeli startup. Especially at the heart of Israeli startup, STARTAU. We are to compete the brightest minds of Israel fairly. With them, Koreans need to co-found a startup in the stage of Silicon Valley.

I have made the plan ready with TAU and I am preparing the plan with Korean visionaries. The key to global startup is in person. I have closed the deal with TAU in regards to this plan. Joseph Klafter and Giora Yaron of TAU are one of the closest relationships I have with Israelis. I have their words to help Koreans to launch in Silicon Valley.

However the issue is that there is a lack of enthusiasm in Korea's government and universities. I want to ask a question. Is there a global startup model in Korea? If no, why not? The reason is simple. There is no reliable infrastructure or mentors to launch global startup in Silicon Valley. Because we lack understanding for global startup ecosystem.

Dov Moran, the inventor of USB, always advises me that he is ready to help young startups referenced by me by bridging important VCs and advisers in Silicon Valley to them. So I am looking for young visionaries who are capable of global startup at the same time training them. The connectors for this project are none other than President Joseph Klafter and Chairman Giora Yaron.

Israeli Ambassadors in South Korea

I have met three Israeli ambassadors since 2011, the year when I first discovered world's power, Israel. I still look back memories I had with them. The reason I am writing this is because I have met the third Israeli ambassador 'Chaim Choshen'. In the 69th anniversary of Israel was the 55th anniversary of Korea and Israel's relation and I had a meeting with him in 'Hyatt Hotel' in Namsan.

The first Israeli ambassador I met was 'Tuvia Israeli'. I had a modest and kind impression about him. With ambassador Tuvia, I first held the first Korea Israel Business Forum and held banquet for the former Prime Minister Ehud Olmert with Korea's young entrepreneurs. He actively helped to bridge our group with Israel.

Without the help of ambassador Tuvia, there won't be Korea Israel Business Council nor Korea Israel Business Forum. In Park Geun-hye administration, government enterprises and organizations had been benchmarking Israel's startup economy. However I had speculated that this strategy would not last very long. Because there are not many who have a profound understanding about history and philosophy about both countries.

There are many chicken franchise businesses trending in South Korea because it is believed to make large profit. At the beginning of Park Geun-hye administration, most of Korea's business forums and seminars were about Israeli startup. However, how many out of them still have in contact with Israel's expertise network and global startup leaders?

I had been fighting a lonely fight. I was not funded by government but only worked with civil corporations and formed relationship with Israeli global leadership network and held business forums and endorsed MOU. To accomplish Korea and Israel relation only by civil efforts, I was busy every single day for the last 7 years. I studied and investigated extra hours in order to catch up with Israel's global leadership and wrote thousands of emails to them.

The first man who taught me the spirit of 'Hutzpa' was Israeli ambassador, 'Tuvia'. He was kindly invited us as their business partner and through him, many networks with Israeli government enterprises and global multination corporations were bridged. With his kindness, ambassador 'Tuvia' was truly a great supporter of Korea and Israel relation.

Second Israeli ambassador was 'Uri Shraga GUTMAN'. Before coming to South Korea, he was former Israeli ambassador in Taiwan and he is very acknowledged about Asian cultures. When he was assigned a role in South Korea, it was probably when South Korea was most interested in Israel. All seminars and international forums were held during his second term. He was corporate-friendly ambassador.

I held Korea Israel Business Forum with him. I invited Israeli international entrepreneurs who are introduced in the book of Startup Nation in Hyatt Hotel. The 2nd Korea Israel Business Forum was with Minister Han Jeong-hwa of Ministry of SMEs and Startups and Minister Yoon Jong-rok of Ministry of Science, ICT and Future Planning and the forum was largely promoted by ambassador 'Uri Shraga GUTMAN' to be successful.

With this chance, the 3rd and 4th Israel Business Forum was also successful. Without the help of ambassador 'GUTMAN' and Israel Embassy, there would not be KIBC. These two Israeli ambassadors have different characters but they are both deeply patriotic to Israel.

The third Israeli ambassador is Chaim Choshen. He is a great man with high tolerance for others. He has disabled children thus he is very considerate and interested in policies for disabled people. He seemed like he investigated a lot about Korea. I asked him about Ahn Cheol-soo, one of presidential candidates of Korea. He responded;

'Steve Jobs of South Korea'.

He was smiling outside but he had his Jewish sharpness and cold insight. I was looking forward to building Korea-Israel relation under his term. I admire Israel. There is no other model for South Korea better than Israel. I am not future scientist nor prophet however I have insight and knowledge to read the future.

One can see the future of Korea looking into Israel. Korea and Israel have many things in common in terms of politics, economy and history. If we look closely to Israel's structural innovation of a large corporation, it teaches us that if Korea misses our chance to innovate, we will be enslaved to large corporation system. For this reason, I am pro-Israel. I want to introduce Israel's global network to Korea's government, entrepreneurs and leaders.

Why? There are some questions I ask myself before I do what I do

1. Am I the only one who is eligible for this role?
2. Do I have firm worldview and philosophy about my job?

I have a role as an expert of Israel that I am forever grateful for.

Korean government and corporations were ignorant towards Israel. Israel was a distanced foreign country to Korea. Why? There has been false prejudice and wrong attempts towards Israel. This was a good opportunity for me to become Israel expert. However we need to see this opportunity at a national level. For Korea to survive the global economic war, Korea needs help of global Jewish network.

If we look at former US president Trump, he is not afraid of anything. But there is one thing that Trump is afraid of. It is when it comes to making policies about Jewish people. Trump grew up in New York. New York is literally Jewish America. It's the world of Jews. Finance, real estates are all owned by Jews. Former president Trump always lived with Jews and did business with them.

▲ Together with Israeli Ambassador to South Korea Haim Choshen.

A senior adviser and Minister of Finance of White House are Jews. He is constantly surrounded by Jews. However Korea is not paying enough attention to this important fact. American president is grown up in a Jewish background and is making Jewish networks and policies. What should Koreans do? We need to get close to Jews. We need to play with Jews. We need to eat, exchange and do business with them.

I wish all the best for the Israeli Ambassador, Chaim Choshen. I am looking forward to building a dream stage with Israel and Korea. Therefore I am taking deep breath. I do not hurry for I know those figures in Israel who are pro-Korea will help me. I am going to introduce global Jewish network to South Korea with him. I am looking forward to the new era of Chaim Choshen.

Israel Project for Globlal Startup of Geyonggido

In September 2017, when the national holiday was about to start, I got a call. It was from Gyeonggido Assembly. It was a sudden meeting request from Kotra (S&M Business Global Accelerating Organization) located in Gwanggyo. This meeting was the initiation of the field trip to Israel's startup ecosystem one the month later. Through many approaches with administrative officers, Gyeonggido Assembly finally started noticing Israeli startup model for successful global acceleration.

After final meeting with Kang Deuk-gu Deputy Governor, Team leader of coalition office in charge, director Son Byeong-jun of Gyeonggi Center for Creative Economy & Innovation we headed over to Israel. This trip was more meaningful because this trip was accompanied with policy makers of Gyeonggido startup. As signifiant as this meeting was, I was able to hold meetings with some significant figures from Israeli politics and international corporations.

This trip was fundamental groundwork for Korea startups to launch globally. We investigated the startup ecosystem of Israel and how it is different to Korea, Israel's exceptional strategies to acquire global competence and how to launch a startup as a result of Korea-Israel collaboration.

There is innovation hub called SOSA in Israel. It was founded by VCs and investors of Israel, which makes SOSA more outstanding than other accelerators. SOSA is more than a startup accelerator but a platform for startup innovation. Since 2012, SOSA is my mandatory stopping spot for visitors from Korea's government, startup universities, corporations in every visit to Israel.

SOSA is where global startup starts. Every time I hold Korea Israel Business Forum in Israel, I make a visit to SOSA to show why Israeli startups are global. Startups throughout the world come to SOSA to get educated and to launch their startups globally through SOSA's network.

There is also another national organization called Israel Innovation Authority (IIA). IIA was previously called OCS which was a global startup incubation center under former prime minister of Israel and is now reformed to IIA. OCS that led Israel's global startups in the past is innovated as IIA that will incubate new Israeli global startups.

After collapse of the USSR, OCS was an organization for creating startup policies for the brightest minds of the Ashkenazi Jews and creating successful startup programs. OCS is now reconstituted to IIA as an independent government institution that enables startup policies enforcement in order to create future industries, which is operated by an Israeli civil group. This unique structure of IIA shows Israeli's unique business style to operate a national global startup incubating center.

After 3 days trip in Israel, director Son Byeong-jun of Gyeonggi Center for Creative Economy & Innovation stated these words in the flight back to South Korea;

> "It was amazing to see why Israel's global startups are so powerful as I had heard of. When I go back to South Korea, I will make efforts to benchmark Israel's startup model for the growth of Korea's global startup."

There is a Korean saying,

> "Only those who tried meat knows how to eat delicious meat."

Likewise, only those who experienced global business knows global business. Israel is a pathway to the sky. The Roman Empire attempted to destroy Israelis who revolted against them and felt so threatened by them that Rome decided to scatter people of Israel all throughout the world. And Jews lived as refugees wandering around the foreign lands for two millennials.

Although Jews were scattered around the world as diasporas for 2,000 years, they had not forsaken their national identity by preserving their language and culture that they regained their homeland after 2,000 years and managed to establish Israel as a nation once again in the history. Now Israel is dominating world's finance, real estate and IT industries. How did Israel conquer their territory that was once wiped out of the world map and become the world's most powerful nation?

It is 'desperation'. Deficiency of resources, country, homeland, oil and

▲ Together with Kang Deuk-gu, former Vice Governor of Gyeonggi Province (currently a member of the Democratic Party of Korea), at the headquarters of SOSA Korea.

even after re-establishment of a nation, it's still a small land of small population. There are more disadvantages than advantages for the nation of Israel. However Israel has overcome its shortcomings. They didn't complain nor despair but desperately persisted their goals.

Trip to Israel in 2017 was very meaningful to me. I also had to put up with the harsh reality of Korea's indifference towards Israel but tried my best to make Israel known to Korea's entrepreneurs, universities and government institutions for seven years. I have endorsed many MOUs between two nations, however Korea was way too behind to be a reliable business partner with Israel. However it is also too early to disappoint.

Yesterday, Gyeonggi Center for Creative Economy & Innovation and Korean Telecoms (KT) asked for another trip to Israel for affiliation with

SOSA. This was accomplishment after 7 months work of persuasion and it was accomplishment of spirit of Hutzpha to be exact. Blood of Israel is in me, I think I am at least half Israeli.

CHAPTER 02

Global Israel
KKUMERS

Former Startup Israel Prime Minister, Yehud Olmert

I have never imagined of meeting one country's VIP, especially not of my own country but Israel's. I can still recall the day I met Prime Minister of Israel vividly. In 9th March 2012, I invited colleagues for the visitation of Prime Minister, Ehud Olmert at Hyatt Hotel. Many were marveled at this unexpected encounter.

I happened to know that prime minister Ehud Olmert was coming to 'Asia Leaders Conference' hosted by Chosen Media. At that time, I got to know Korea"s adviser for prime minister Ehud Olmert. The president of the Korean Association of State of Israel introduced him to me. I

▲ Together with former Prime Minister Ehud Olmert.

offered him to introduce the leaders of Korean venture companies of next generation. This offer was approved by prime minister Ehud Olmert and I got an invitation emailed to me signed by prime minister Ehud Olmert.

Since that moment, identification assessment of me underwent by Korean government officials, Israeli ambassadors and by staff in the foreign affairs department of the Seoul Metropolitan Police Department who were appointed as his security guards. I got a call everyday from government to ensure invitees list which took a lot of formal process and efforts. It was not a simple job to host a conference bringing economic leaders from both countries together in the presence of the Prime Minister of Israel.

When I look back at this event, I am even surprised by myself to have had courage to host such a big conference. But I believed in the value of learning from Israel by building long-term relationship for Korea's next economic leaders. From South Korea, we invited young venture capitalists and government persons.

This group of young Korean CEOs were; CEO Lee Si-won of Siwon English School CEO Park Hyun-woo of InnoRed CEO Kim Jong-suk of Hello Kitty CEO Lim Young-seo of Porridge Story CEO Lee Seon-yong of Asian Star.

who are now CEOs of medium-sized enterprises. They all underwent business management classes within the same community and are now having business conference with former prime minister, Ehud Olmert.

Members of the National Music(Gugak) Orchestra, singers of Seoul National University College of Music, minister Kim Hyeon-jong of FTA minister of Trade, president Lee Geong-suk of Sookmyung Women's University, these were the invitees of South Korea who co-shared our vision for Korea and Israel to promote relation of two nations. This meaningful day turned into a great success. After meeting with Korea's young leaders, former prime minister, Ehud Olmert invited us to Israel.

This marks the historical beginning of Korea-Israel business relation. There are still some obstacles that exist to discuss K-I relation through official diplomacy channel. Especially, one cannot forsake business relation with Middle Eastern countries that has oil money. However business relation between civil corporations does not need government interference.

By this, the unknown future arrived before my eyes. I had a life's chance to

▲ Having dinner with former Prime Minister Ehud Olmert at the King David Hotel.

get to know VIPs of Israel. Most leaders in the world are Jews. Especially politics and finance leaders are dominated by Jews. I have an opportunity to become the expert of Jewish network in Korea.

Since that moment, unimaginable events have come to my life. It was something that I had never dreamt to happen in my life. I have become the connector who bridges startups of both countries to advance startup ecosystem and economy through emails and phone calls with VIPs of Israel. The future is often full of unexpected.

Encounter with Israel, former prime minister Ehud Olmert, World dominating Israeli leaders were all of unexpected future. However these unexpected relationships have come to my life suddenly. And I do not let them go in my life. Important thing is that you need to be thoroughly ready for your vision.

My parents who sent me to the USA for education, mentors I met in the States, business experiences of my own in Korea, all played a fundamental role to lay a foundation for my dream. I have never felt anxious or intimidated by global leaders. I thank CREATOR of Israel, my parents, great mentors and colleagues who have me to trained in ideology and excessiveness.

Dreams come true when one is ready. If I was not ready for my dream, even opportunities come, they would not be mine. It is pointless to challenge something when one does not have ability to manage the task. I want to say this to young generation of Korea.

"Can your preparedness be assessed objectively?"

It's not easy. It could take pain and struggle. However once passing the tunnel of struggle, opportunities come and dreams come true. Let's turn our eyes outside the box. Korea is narrow and complex land but the world is large and has many things to do. Now, let's challenge our dreams of life.

▲ Former Prime Minister Ehud Olmert at the Grand Hyatt Hotel party dinner.

Former Chairman of Tel Aviv University, Giora Yaron

I was able to meet Israeli global entrepreneurs leaders at the first Kore Israel business forum. Among them was legendary venture CEO, chair of TAU, Giora Yaron. His first impression was very strong. A blonde man with manly physical who had an overwhelming charisma. He seemed like an ideal leader.

I was amazed by his career path which I searched in the internet. He is a successful serial entrepreneur who endorsed more than ten M&As with international corporations in the USA and is still a legendary entrepreneur

▲ With Giora Yaron, Chairman of Tel Aviv University's Board of Directors.

of Israeli startup scene. Generally speaking, one success in M&A is already considered a huge business success. However he succeeded M&A for ten times in Silicon Valley and NASDAQ, which makes him an excellent CEO.

Some of his successful M&A cases includes well-known global corporations of the USA including Cisco and HP who bought his startups. It was a golden opportunity to have met CEO Giora Yaron. He has bridged some of influential figures of Israeli global entrepreneurs for network and affiliation with Korea since the first Korea Israel Business Forum.

If I didn't meet CEO Giora Yaron, I would not have become an expert of Israel. He has helped me more than he needed to. He has been enthusiastically solved any issues I was having with networking with Israel. He was out of my league who was already a legendary venture star CEO.

Israel has holiday days that are equal to six months period of time annually. They take their work off during the Biblical appointed times. All the holiday seasons take good six months out of the whole year. So it takes a lot of patience to do business with Israel. You can never reach them in their holiday seasons. One might find Israel hard to do business in.

November last year, I was preparing for a trip to Israel however this schedule was overlapped with feast of tabernacles, Sukkot. This trip was to make a cooperation model between universities of Korea and Israel and it needed endorsement of MOU between institutions. For this, I was making contact to Israel, without knowing that it was Sukkot. When Giora Yaron took my call, he explained about the feast of tabernacles.

At that moment, I was in a panic. The situation in Korea made the November trip inevitable. So I explained the situation of Korea and asked him for a favor. For MOU endorsement, it needed documents signed which takes complex processes. Especially, it needs to be carefully assessed by lawyers to ensure legal terms and effects on both sides. I found out later that for this endorsement, Israelis had to labour during the feast of Tabernacles. I was very thankful for this.

A person needs his ability to succeed but relationships are more important. I have a special standard in a relationship. When I need to meet someone, I do not make unnatural connection nor try to approach people who are close to the desirable person. I patiently wait in a belief that destiny will bring desirable relationships rather than making approaches by force.

Giora Yaron and I are a good example my notion. I did not try to get to know him neither did he need to get to know me. We were destined to meet to bridge between both nations. It is such a blessing to have been connected with him in regards to Israel. I am looking forward to future; the future of Korea and Israel, which will be built together with Giora Yaron.

CEO of Yozma Fund, Yigal Erlich

Israel is a startup nation. Startup means building a country in a broad sense. How Israel became a startup nation is largely contributed by former Prime Minister Ehud Olmert who established national policies of startups, which was co-built by civil and government enterprises.

In that sense, Israeli startup model, which is led by civil enterprises and supported by government institution that resulted in great accomplishments, is a model, which was never attempted by any other nation other than Israel and it will be a good example for Korea. The book 'Startup Nation' was

▲ With Chairman Yigal Erlich.

endorsed by the former Prime Minister, Ehud Olmert. This book explains policies that were enforced by Ehud Olmert when he was Prime Minister to accelerate Israeli startups.

Among these policies, the core startup ecology system is backed by VC. If venture capital does not support startups, they cannot do anything. Because most startups lack seed money. Innovative technology, idea and drive are good tactics for a startup but at the end of the day, it's the 'money' that will make the startup's product come to reality.

For Israel to become a startup nation, they built VC network as the core body of their startup ecosystem. The former Prime Minister Ehud Olmert raised fund from Israeli entrepreneurs in overseas and Israeli government to found 'YOZMA Fund' as the venture capital for startup. The CEO of YOZMA Fund is Yigal Erlich. When I met him in Israel, I had an impression that he is an international giant of marketing.

Most Israelis are skilled in marketing and sells well at exit. They are great negotiators who can sell a product that has value of five billion as ten billion because of these marketing skills. I had an impression of CEO of YOZMA Fund, Yigal Erlich is born M&A skills person. There is a famous quote that he left for audience of Korea.

In Korea, navigation service 'kimgisa' was sold to KAKAO Inc. by 65 billion and he added the following. Similar case is in Israel. Israeli navigation service 'Waze Mobile' was sold to google by 1.6 trillion won. What is the difference? Waze Mobile was sold to global multinational corporation and 'kimgisa' was sold to a national company, KAKAO. 'kimgisa' was developed as Korea's navigation service and WAZE Mobile was developed as a global mobile navigation service. That is the difference.

1.6 trillion VS 65 billion..this is the reality of Korea and Israel M&A market. They both sold same mobile navigation service but the sales price difference is enormous. This difference is made by VC capacity. There is no global VC in Korea. However in Israel, there are many global VCs who can negotiate with Silicon Valley.

'YOZMA Fund' used to be the frontlet VC of Israel. The CEO Yigal Erlich pioneered and flourished YOZMA Fund. He is the most prominent VC that I have ever met. He leads negotiations to be advantageous for Israel and execute the deals successfully. South Korea needs to build global VCs as YOZMA Fund. If we don't, we will be boiling frogs in the global startup world.

▲ Dinner Event Former Israeli Prime Minister Ehud Olmert in Israel.

CEO of RAD Group, Zohar Zisapel

Israel does not have large corporations like Korea. Israel's system of a large corporation is designed to be ruled by two entities to prevent corporative dominance over the nation of Israel but the nation to rule over the corporation instead. The more you investigate Israel's startup ecosystem, you would admire it even more. Because Israel is such a small nation. However the world is dominated by Jewish Americans.

Among many Israeli global corporations, I would like to point out an outstanding global company. It is RAD Group. The RAD Group is led by CEO 'Zohar Zisapel'. This photo was taken in his office. He had a modest

▲ With RAD Group's Chairman, Zohar Zisapel.

appearance just like any other middle-aged man. However once engaged in a conversation with him, one would soon find out that he is a giant business man.

Let's look at the RAD Group. RAD Group is Israel's frontline telecommunication company. RAD Group has a global distribution channel that sells telecommunication devices to 56 countries all around the world. About three of RAD Group owned startups were successfully listed in NASDAQ. RAD Group is small yet a powerful global IT telecommunication company. RAD Group manages 23 of its own sub companies and critically analyzes past and future to measure the best

▲ 'Thinking Man' statue by Rodin displayed at the entrance of the RAD Group headquarters.

▲ A work by the world-renowned artist Andy Warhol displayed at the RAD Group information desk.

timing to invest in or sell stocks while managing RAD Group as a whole. For example, even they have a highly profitable business, if it is assessed to hold not enough value in the future, they sell such businesses without hesitation. On the other hand, if a business constantly needs investment but is estimated to hold ensuing value in the future, RAD Group pays the price of sacrifice and investment.

You will encounter something impressive when you enter the RAD Group building. There is a world's masterpiece statue The Thinker by Auguste Rodin in his company lobby. I fist thought it was imitation but I soon found out that it is authentic artwork. With this masterpiece, there are more paintings of world's heritage hung near the information desk at the lobby, which are guarded by security guards at all times.

The first picture is the office by CEO 'Zohar Zisapel'. It is located high,

overlooking TEL Aviv park. He invited me over to his office and while I was posing to take a picture with him, I touched his statue by accident. He jokingly said
"you almost broke statue worth three billion"
and it gave me shimmers on my spine. He was not just a wealthy man, he had a great sense of art.

Every time I visit Israel, he always invites me to his office and we share a good meal. One of his favorite restaurant is Hudson steak house, which serves one of the best steaks in the world. I am very happy when I meet Zohar because he is down to earth who has insight to read the future. I have never imagined of myself being friend with him. This is the moment that dreams truly come true.

▲ In the office of Zohar Zisapel the chairman of RAD Group, with a professor from the Prime Business Unit of Ewha Womans University and the head of the Startup Support Center at Busan Dongseo University.

Father of Israel's Startup, Yossi Vardi

Anyone who is in Israel's startup industry calls his, the father of startup. He is the Israel's global startup legend with no explanation needed. He is an expert venture investor and founder. Israel's most prominent global venture capital is Sequoia Capital. Many global success stories in Silicon Valley are the startups that have been invested by Sequoia Capital.

Google, Oracle, Youtube and Apple are legendary Silicon Valley stories who were invested by global ventures that turned into great success. Knowing that Sequoia Capital is Israel owned, it is self-explanatory that why startups in Israel are global. As Silicon Valley is the center of world's startups, it is 'Yossi Vardi' who immigrated Silicon Valley to Tel Aviv Israel and amused the world with his successful investment in startups.

As anyone knows, Israel is a startup nation. It's a small nation of 7 million population surrounded by 1.3 billion middle eastern population and this small country is located at the verge of seashore. However this small nation is shaking the world. Especially in Korea, Israel is known as 'middle eastern bomb'. Despite of all Israel's disadvantages, Israel is making the world's most fortune and influential leaders.

The present CEO of Facebook is Mark Zuckerberg who is also

Israeli. One can name a list of successful Israeli startups and venture names endlessly. As much so, there are numerous successful global entrepreneurs that Israel came forth. Korea is not very aware of Israel's global leadership. To know one Israeli leader means to build network with global leaders.

One of the Israeli global startup leaders that Korea is not very aware of is 'Yossi Vardi'. He is a skilled global startup investor who for the last 40 years, he invested in 60 high tech companies and successfully executed them. The reason he is still called the father of Israel startup is that he is still an influential figure to young entrepreneurs.

How I have come to know him was through hosting Korea Israel Business Forum. He is still an enthusiastic visionary who encourages innovation of startups of for the next generations. Growing 60 international companies in 40 years shows how passionate he is towards startups.

Many Korea's business men invest in real estates to become building owners. It is quite challenging for Korean businesses to maintain sustainability. Statistics show that 90% of KOSDAQ listed companies go bankrupt. Koreans are faced to do business with low business life expectancy.

Perhaps, this is why many Korean corporations are trying to escape through exit after being listed in KOSDAQ. However that is unlike case in Israel and USA. There are more cases of serial startups. They do not settle down at one time success but continues challenging in new startups and those who succeed in serial startups are considered real business success. Where successful business men generally end up as building owners, in Korea, it is a rare case in Israel and USA. Why is that? It's because of the spirit of Hutzpha.

This is why 'Yossi Vardi' is the father of Israel startup. He is an international figure who succeeded in serial startups of 60 startups in 40 years. He still invests in startups in Tel Aviv, Israel. Through global conference DLD, he is a unique business figure in the world stage. It is life opportunity for me to have met global startup legend, 'Yossi Vardi'.

The point of global startup is simple. It is to be assessed globally in Silicon Valley, USA. Korea is still a boiling frog who has not set an outstanding example of global startup. Korea's global partner is no other than Israel. Because Korea cannot survive in Silicon Valley by itself.

Because Silicon Valley is ruled by Jewish Startup Mafia. It is a league of Israeli investors. No one can easily penetrate into the field. They are highly skilled at incubating startups to exit within their global network. It is a unique market that excels in boosting corporative values for resale.

From this perspective, it is impossible for Korean startups to break in. If we objectively assess our current situation, we don't deserve to be part of that league. Because Israelis already set their own investment rules, which makes it hard for other investors to penetrate in. There is no room for Korea to break in the high walls of Silicon Valley.

▲ Together with Yoshi Bardi at the 3rd KIBF.

However there is one thing that I realized after networking with Israeli startup investors' mafia circle. If Korea takes indirect approach, Korea can also come up successful entrepreneurs in Silicon Valley, which is co-founding with Israel. Even if we own less share, it will be historic if we co-found with Israelis.

Israeli venture capitals cannot invest in Korea's startups. They have investment principles. Israel's biggest investment companies like Pitango or JVP can only invest in Israeli startups based in Silicon Valley. So I have a vision to co-found with global venture investors like 'Yossi Vardi'.

Before I became an Israel expert, I was a foreigner to startup. However networking with Israel's VIPs, I have become startup expert. Especially, I was able to communicate with Israel's global leaders, who have influence in Israel. I have become in contact with VVIPs of VIPs of Israel. Through this network, I have learned why Israelis do global business.

The problem with Korea's startup is that it's not global. Like boiling frogs, we compete internally. Like Israel, we ought to launch in global market and come up with global entrepreneurs. The network I've been building with Israeli VIPs will meet its best moment.

'Yossi Vardi'. he is the father of startup. Through him, I have come to know his global network. When he moves, Silicon Valley moves. Investing with him in a startup will mean it will become a global startup. Like Israel, we need to incubate global startups. With this dream, I discuss co-founding a startup with him. I hope the day when Korea and Israel co-found a startup would come soon.

General Secretary of Technion University, Peres Ravi

One of the goals of Park Geun-hye administration was to win Nobel Prize. There was a committee board formed with the brightest minds in the science field and other experts to achieve Nobel Prize. The photo of one of KIBC members, chairman Choi Jin-seong sitting next to president Park Geun-hye was pressed in the newspaper. Koreans have a way of rushing things; they have to have things done as quickly as instant noodle. This is reflected in their desire to win Nobel prize according to their pace.

▲ With General Secretary Peres Ravi.

Do you know 40% of Nobel Prize winners are Jewish? These Jewish winners include those who dwell in Israel and diasporas throughout the world. Israel has only population of 7 million. However Israeli diasporas who were scattered all over the world for 2,000 years have already lived their lives globally.

In order to live in a foreign country, one has to thoroughly adopt culture, history and politics of their migrated country and get along with host citizens. However, Jews, on the other hand, dominate the economy in their migrated country. Especially in Europe and USA, all figures in wealth and academia are Israelis. Although they were without homeland, they turned this disadvantage into their unique strength by forming a global network.

I want to discuss Israeli network that will be practical in today's academia

▲ Kinemaster CEO Lim Il-taek asking a question to Technion's President Peres Ravi.

and business. Especially, I want to discuss Nobel Prize which Koreans are so eager to accomplish. Specifically, in the nomination areas of physics and chemistry where the contribution towards humanity is recognized worldwide instead of nomination area of peace. Why has Korea been excluded all these years?

Does it become possible if government organizes a special committee of board to win Nobel Prize? I hate to point out that Korea still stays in the past of Park Chung-hee administration era. His leadership was suitable for that time of the past. However the present economic situation is not at a development stage but the current economic situation is seeking for sustainability to stay listed as one of top developed countries.

Politician 'Woo Byung-woo' is a monster figure that reflects only negative sides of Park Chung-hee era. In today's generation, it is all

▲ Technion University President Peres Ravi giving a lecture at the 3rd KIBF.

about embracing diversity and individualism to celebrate creative society we live in. Uniformed education system will never earn Nobel Prize to Korean nation. When I was in middle and high school, I had to shave my head, beaten by teachers, scorned if I rose any questions and had to wear school uniform.

There were no vibrant colors such as red, yellow or orange in Korea's education environment in the past. Korea's education system was based on uniformity, memorization, repetition like a machine and how much has it changed over time? Korea's machine-like education system has not changed much as its whole purpose focuses on entering universities. Therefore it is ironic that one expects Nobel Prize out of this machine like education system that eliminates any form of creativeness and imaginativeness.

▲ The president of Technion University Peres Ravi, giving a lecture at the 3rd KIBF (Korea-Israel Business Forum).

If a nation doesn't change education, nothing will change. Especially, if one wants to win a Nobel Prize, there needs to be a solid academic foundation for basic science. This will not be the case if Korea sill persists in education style of the past which are prior learning and memorization. Technion University of Technology in Israel is a very small in size but their education system came forth four Nobel Prize winners. It's because they have strong education basics.

Moreover, Technion University is very pro-corporation. It has a well-balanced infrastructure of government, corporations and university that connects and supports each other for a thorough investigation of any given task. If one investigator is deceased without concluding his investigation, it will not affect investigation processs. Investigators are only there to investigate. If a professor is deceased during his investigation, the next person in charge will take the tern to continue in the investigation.

USB inventor Dov Moran also went to Technion. In 2015, he gave me a special gift from Israel. He gave me the book '25 innovations for human' published by international IT magazine, Accenture. He shared with me that this book was given to him the day before meeting with me and he only had one copy, but he wanted to give it to me as a gift. I felt flattered to know that I have become a good friend of global startup legend of Israel.

1. Greenhouse
2. Energy & Peak oil
3. Medicine

4. Informatiom

5. Pharmaceuticals

6. Food & Water

7. Peace

This book was published by world's top experts, scientists, inventors of their expertise. These 25 Technion University graduates are the authors of 'Innovations for Human' and this shows why Technion University graduates have won Nobel Prize for four times.

I have endorsed one MOU between Korea and Israeli governments and universities before. However the problem always seems to come next. Once MOU is endorsed, the next step requires further communication, which is not met by Korea's end. Frankly speaking, Korea cannot catch up with Israel's capacity. Communication needs to be done mutually but Korea's professors and students simply cannot catch up with Israel's level.

More honestly, I have an impression that Korean government and universities just needed documental evidence that they endorsed with globally well-known institutions and universities of Israel as a trophy to include in their portfolio. Once this document is gained, Korea's government or universities no longer make efforts to further network with Israel. I don't want to be the puppet of their administrative strategies. Korea needs to change.

Worldly professors and leaders need to come forward from Korea like

Technion University. I am searching for the eligible candidate among the next presidential candidates who could globally build economic and educational network and co-work with other global leaders. Korea cannot afford to be a boiling frog any longer. Being number one in Korea means nothing anymore. It is a sinking boat like 'SEWOL'.

Korea needs to develop KAIST as a global education institution, benchmarking Technion University of Technology. Our young generation needs to grow as global leaders who can compete in USA and other developed countries. The more I look back, it is life's chance to have come to know the Jewish network. Many people knock on the door of USA and China, now knowing who the dark horse really is.

I want to introduce Israeli network to Korea. But I don't want to be a puppet, manipulated by vain agendas of public institutions. If we do not grasp the essence now, we will end up copying others. Chair of Technion University of Technology is my friend. We have known each other for a long time and he is pro-Korea. However the problem is Technion does not have partner in Korea. When will Koreans be connected to Israel in a real way?

President of Startup VC Pitango, Nechemia Peres

The first time I met him was when I invited him as a main speaker to Korea Israel Business Forum. He is a representative of Israel's startup ecosystem as the founder of VC, Pitango. He is also son of former Prime Minister 'Shimon Peres', who is the founding father of Israel. 'Nechemia Peres' was reported in the press when his father passed away and his father's death was mourned by many VIPs of the world.

The former president of USA Barack Obama attended the funeral to comfort him, which was photographed in the JoongAng Media. Nechemia Peres is now a CEO of Israel's biggest VC and directs

▲ Together with Nechemia Peres, Chairman of the Peres Center for Peace and Innovation.

▲ With Giora Yaron, Tel Aviv University Board of Directors Chairman, and Nechemia Peres Pitango Capital Chairman, in front of the Second Temple tunnel.

Pitango's investment. There is an episode that I want to share about Nechemia Peres that reflects his excellent management tactics in running Pitango. Once I visited the second tunnel of Military Demarcation Line in South Korea with visitors from Israel. The trip was accompanied with Giora Yaron and we went to the very edge of the border of North Korea.

Guiding their trip in Korea, I asked him many questions that I was curious about. I asked him what the greatest thing about Israel's startup ecosystem was. He responded without hesitation. The greatest asset about Israel's startup ecosystem is 'Hutzpha spirit' which is the entrepreneurship of Israel.

'Hutzpha' is often translated as shamelessness, reckless, daring which is the unique entrepreneurship of Israel. The person who is equivalent to this expression in Korea would be CEO Jeong Ju-young and apparently Israel has many entrepreneurs like Jeong Ju-young. There is a famous saying of now past CEO Jeong Ju-young.

"Have you tried it until it succeeds?"

The foundation of Israeli entrepreneurship is invincible will. In Korea, we have only a few entrepreneurs who founded global corporation like 'Jeong Ju-young' with invincible will but in Israel all startup founders work with Hutzpha spirit. After hearing his response, I looked somewhat puzzled.

Because I expected his response to be something like 'logical system of Israeli ecosystem'. However his response was Hutzpha spirit. Then I asked him the second question.

I asked him why Israel's startups are so successful. Then he responded with

▲ Barack Obama, former President of the United States, comforting a grieving Nechemia Peres, Chairman of Pitango Venture Capital, during the funeral of President Shimon Peres (source: JoongAng Media).

the VC structure behind Israeli startups. In Israel, one can found a startup without money. What it takes is invincible will and brilliant idea and if anyone has those qualities, he can be without money. As he was telling me about Israeli VC system, he then told me about the principles of Israeli investment. Anyone is given equal opportunity and fair competition in Israel.

After initiation stage of investment of receiving seed money, a startup goes through investment of series A, B and C and in these processes of investment, an enormous amount of fund is transacted. There is a fair competition structure where anyone can apply. This lays fervent soil for anyone to expect success from their startups as opportunities are not limited to a few as demonstrated in many of Israel's successful startups.

So I asked him the third question. "What are the principles of Israel's investment?" Asking this question, I let my provocative nature show to

▲ Nechemia Peres, Chairman of Pitango Capital, at the 2nd KIBF (in the Hyatt Hotel).

them. "Your late-father, former Prime Minister, Shimon Peres collected investment capital for one of Israel's startup legend 'Better Place', why didn't you invest in 'Better Place'? This question could be a difficult question for those who are in a startup industry to answer.

Because his late father 'Shimon Peres', the prime minister of Israel, collected investment capital for 'Better Place'. When his late father met CEO 'Shai Agassi' was the beginning of this global startup. He gave me a very simple answer to this question.

> "I used to do business with Agassi in the same building, and of course my late father led investment capital for Agassi's 'Better Place'. This is a fact but it's got nothing to do with me. Investment in Better Place was my father's business, which is totally a separate matter from Pitango's investment standards"

▲ The 2nd Korea-Israel Business Forum (KIBF) Opening Ceremony.

"Why didn't you invest in Better Place?"

He responded firmly. The board members of Pitango all disagreed in investment in Better Place. Even though I am the founder of Pitango who owns most of the share, I cannot make my own decision about management and investment. I thought I have to separate my friendship with Shai Agassi from doing business with him.

I realized many things after this conversation. I realized why Israeli leaders manage global fortune and matters. Israel draws a clear line between personal matters and public matters. I hope Korean leaders to learn Israeli's professional work ethics.

Daewoo Shipbuilding & Marine Engineering became an insolvent enterprise

▲ Nechemia Peres, President of Pitango Venture Capital, discussing with young Korean entrepreneurs at the 2nd KIBF.

because of enormous accounting fraud. According to civilian opinion, it is impossible for the company to revive. Why has Daewoo Shipbuilding & Marine Engineering become an insolvent enterprise? Because they lied to investors by faking their accounting records by enormous statistics. 'Deloitte' was the accountant firm for Daewoo Shipbuilding & Marine Engineering at that time and was supposed to take responsibility for this accident. However, Korea's reality was not quite ideal.

One of high ranking officials in finance told me they only changed the name of accounting firm and all the workers still remained. Why is Korea so inseparable from corruption? Korea's society is still strongly rooted in the network advantaged by academia and relationships. One of current Korea's presidential candidates went to the university.

That university is generally not considered as top universities in Korea. However this university is already getting a lot of attention. There are rumors that the government institutions are already looking after many matters promoted by this university. Why can't Korea form a public system that have strong principles and philosophies? How much of sacrifice and pain of corruption would Korea go through again to fix this problem? We need to ask this question.

Israeli startups are open to everyone fairly. However looking at what Korea's startup ecosystem is like, it leaves me speechless with unbelief. Because people who don't have basic knowledge of startups, seat as the board members of policy making that determines destiny of many Korea's startups. A person who has no experience of founding a startup is the key decision making person. This is like blind man leading the road. Why should we go through this bad cycle?

I look up to Israel's startup ecosystem. This startup ecosystem of fair opportunities lays fervent soil for inventors like Dov Moran to rise. Will Korea have outstanding innovator like Dov Moran? Korea's government should not enforce startup policies without proper knowledge of how to run a startup.

Looking up to Israel's startup ecosystem, I fight my own battle in 'Hapjeong-dong'. Things are accomplished very slowly. However I take a deep breath and do my best everyday. History is not made over night. History is made when people with like-minded vision and philosophy try together for a long time.

For this reason, I do not hurry. Generational leaders are not born but made. Many youngsters come to Hapjeong-dong through words of mouth. I am implementing Israeli startup ecosystem in Hapjeong-dong as a test. Even though I go hungry, mentoring Israeli startup system to Korean youngsters give me joy. Because they are growing.

CEO of Audiocodes, Shabtai Adlersberg

It's not easy to run a conglomerate in Israel. Most businesses in Israel start off as a startup and later get M&A or exits. In other words, it is more usual in Israel to exit at a startup stage than grow it into a long-lived company. For this reason, it is not very common in Israel to do a conglomerate.

However there is a rare case of a conglomerate that can be found in Israel. RAD Group and Audiocodes are these conglomerates that are based in Israel that started off as an IT startup. Audiocodes is a global pioneer in VOIP industry. Audiocodes was founded in 1993 and now has become

▲ With Audiocodes founder Shabtai Adlersberg at Renaissance Hotel in Tel Aviv.

an international VOIP company. It's not easy to maintain world's top position in one industry for over than 25 years. Especially in Israel, where mainstream business is startup, success as a conglomerate is extremely difficult achievement which is astonishing.

Advertising strategies of Audicodes are intriguing. Audiocodes is known for its creativity and uniqueness when it comes to advertisement, that differentiates them from all other telecommunication companies. This shows how unparalleled CEO of Audiocodes is. VOIP is abbreviation of Voice Over Internet Protocol, which is voice communication over internet and VOIP is taking over telephone industry.

The first impression of CEO Shabtai Adlersberg was logical. Before preparing Korea Israel Business Forum, he already knew about us well.

▲ Chairman Shabtai Adlersberg with former KITA Chairman Choi Jin-seong in Korea.

Moreover, he also knew the Israeli board members of KIBC very well. He called me once and requested DVD of Israeli speakers.

I was surprised by this unexpected call. Because he is a very busy man as a global leader of Israeli VOIP market. However he was very willing to thoroughly prepare his speech for the forum. He said he wanted to refer other Israeli speakers from 1st and 2nd KIBF to refine his speech. I was deeply touched.

Finally, I got to meet him in person at Renaissance Hotel located in Tel Aviv beach. He had a gentle charismatic man. He was a gentle business man with a soft voice. Before his speech, he showed me his presentation document and I was surprised for the second time. He was a professional businessman with thorough preparedness.

▲ Shabtai Adlersberg CEO delivering a lecture at the 3rd KIBF.

Among all Israeli VIPs I have ever met, he was the most prepared business man. He wanted to communicate with Korea. At the right time, Choi Jin-seong CTO (Chief Technical Officer) of SKT was an attendee at the forum. As they were both in the same telecommunication industry, they both had same concerns in common. As I was making care observations at Mr Adlersberg, I found out why Israel is strong at being global.

Domestic market is meaningless in Israel. When one founds a startup, even it involves only one founder, he launches homepage in English first. Global homepage building platform, WIX was also a startup in Israel that became a global platform. I believe Israel's strength in global market penetration made the service into a global business.

In Israel, the scale of business is not very important, this is why there are not many conglomerates in Israel. Everyone desires to do startups in Israel and actively involves in startup business to eventually sell them to conglomerates or M&A. In Korea, this type of business deal is considered a miracle but to Israelis, it's daily news. What is the reason behind this big difference?

In Israel, even when business grows into a successful conglomerate, investing or M&A with other startups is not a special occasion. Because this successful conglomerate was once a startup. It remembers its humble beginning and continues to discover potentials in new startups to invest in. CEO of Audiocodes is a CEO of global conglomerate who does not forget his humble beginning.

Among all Israeli companies with continual growth, Audiocodes is definitely an outstanding one. If a company lacks innovation and reformation in global competition, it will gradually be left behind. Korea has a weakness in global market survival rate. Because Korean companies settle down at domestic success and choose to be a boiling frog.

I still connect business between Korea and Israel and also try to bridge universities between both countries. However the problem is that Korea cannot catch up with Israel for Korea lacks a global mind. Global competence is not gained overnight and without global ecosystem and education, it is impossible for a startup to succeed globally.

In this context, Audiocodes case teaches us a great example; a small startup grew into a global leading conglomerate founded on Israel's Hutzpha spirit of not giving up until they achieve their goals. I want to take more startups and entrepreneurs to Israel and show what global competence really means. Because this is the only way to survive in a vast global market. I want to challenge Korea's young generation.

Vice President of Weizmann Lab, Dr. Mudi Sheves

Doctor Mordechai Shevez reminds me of a man next door. He is easygoing and generous. He always remains calm and does not forget to put a smile on his face. He is an internationally renown chemist, vice president of Weizmann Institute of Science and also a CEO who manages all intellectual properties of Weizmann. The first encounter with him was at the campus of Weizmann. He escorted me to every corner of Weizmann and explained about all the departments. One will only accurately learn why Weizmann has become world's renowned science institute only when he visits the institution. Weizmann was named after

▲ Dr. Mudi Sheves, Vice President of the Weizmann Institute of Science.

the first prime minister of Israel. The first prime minister of Israel was not a politician but a scientist. From his science background, he established Weizmann Institute of Science to transform the desolate land of Israel to technology hub as Israel is now.

Weizmann, now has 200 scientists and the institution provides scholars and bachelor course so students can get a degree. The scientific achievements of Weizmann needs no further explanation. Weizmann earns over two trillion per year from loyalty alone. Weizmann also secures its investigators with life support to continue in their study free from the burden of resolutions.

▲ The background is a picture of the former Israeli President who founded the Weizmann Institute of Science.

▲ Dr. Mudi Sheves, Vice President of the Weizmann Institute of Science.

Then what happens when one of scientists is deceased in the middle of his progress? There is no problem. Because there are junior scientists who can take his turn to continue in the investigation. Israel is science heaven. Scientists in Israel hold a great pride. Israel has a culture that privileges scientists. Weizmann, still, receives great amount of fund from government.

Weizmann is also the center of disciplinary convergence . There are five master's and doctorate Koreans who study in Weizmann. They are becoming one of world's top scientists through Israel's world's renowned basic science, advanced science technology and disciplinary convergence. My only hope is that they would not come back to Korea after their study in Weizmann but to continue to build their career in the field of Israel or USA.

Because coming back to Korea, will take away the disciplinary convergence that they once indulged in Israel by Korea's many customs and social order. It is more advantageous for them to come back to South Korea after earning their names in the authoritative of science. Because Korea's society is still abused by traditions, customs and orders.

In Weizmann, they offer students to study different categories of basic science such as chemist, physics and pharmaceutical etc. Unlike Korean university, where students are to choose one expertise, Weizmann students freely crossover different expertises of science during their investigation. This is very important as Israel is one of the best countries for inventing high performing medical devices. This is due to Israel's education system that supports collaboration between engineers and scientists as they share the same lab and coproduce a product.

Doctor Mordechai Shevez is worldly renowned chemist. He is also CEO of

▲ Dr. Mudi Sheves, Vice President of the Weizmann Institute of Science, discussing with young Korean entrepreneurs at the Weizmann Institute of Science.

Weizmann who manages all Weizmann's intellectual properties. Although he seems like a kind man next door, after one hour of conversation with him, you will realize that he is a tough businessman. He always engages in a conversation with smiles but he is armed with numbers and data.

It's been six years since I have built friendship with him. Every time I visit Israel, he always hosts guests from Korea with great intimacy unless he is out overseas. He escorts the crowd and gives explanations in person. He's been a great support to Korea and Israel's relation promoted by Korea Israel Business Council, that myself serve as general secretary. He is an expert of Israel's science and ambassador and pro-Korea Israeli who loves Korea.

Last year November, I visited Weizmann with two professors of Prime Business Group of Ewha Womans University and Head of Business Start-up Support Group of Dongseo University of Busan. This visit was an academic inspection and had nothing to do with business. However he was kind enough to introduce former vice president of Weizmann, professor

David and treated Korea's guests so kindly. He was so genuinely kind to welcome even people who are not business-related.

Israelis have special business DNA to their bones. They don't expect short term outcomes. Once trust is built, that trust lasts lifetime for a lifetime business. However Israelis do not trust people easily. Their trust is usually built after a thorough assessment of the person. This process is sometimes painstakingly tiring and hard, but once it is endured, you will have Jewish network.

Koreans are said to have 'pot nature'. It means it boils quickly and cools quickly. This expression points out Koreans' weakness to have a short sighted vision and high temper. I tried very hard for three years to build network with Israelis. One of Israelis who gave me constant support was Israeli VIP, doctor Mordechai Shevez. What is the most urgent thing for Korea as a developed country?

I believe it is Korea needs to be a country where scientists are well respected. All developed countries highly value scientists. It is not exaggerating to say a destiny of a nation is at the hands of scientists. When scientists devout their intellects to advance scientific technology of a society, all the benefits return to the nation and its citizens. Therefore I believe doctor Mordechai Shevez is also a VIP of South Korea who is pro-Korea Israeli scientist who can set a good example for Korea's science to globally advance.

I believe this network I have with him is a precious asset for Korea. They are global leaders of science. Networking with them is a tremendous step up for Korea's next scientific advancement. We are to use their global network to advance our nation. One cannot foresee the future without Israelis. There is a saying 'All road leads to Rome' but I want to say 'All road is through Israelis'. Challenge yourself to Israeli network!

Nobel Prize Winner, Professor Robert Aumann

It was at the first Korea Israel Business Forum in 2012 when I first met him. He appeared to the event with his shining silver hair. In the venue, the former Prime Minister of Israel, 'Ehud Olmert' was giving a speech. At his entrance, the former Prime Minister stopped his speech to make his presence known by introducing professor Robert J. Aumann. I was surprised by this scene. During 'Ehud Olmert's speech, he honored Aumann and showed his intimate relationship with him by calling him by his name and their casual friendship was noticed by his jokes towards Aumann. Israel is a practical country. Israel is open for Prime Minister and professor to call

▲ In Robert Aumann's office at the Hebrew University.

each other by name and build friendship despite of social status.

He was born in Frankfurt am Main in German, 8th of June 1930. He migrated to New York, USA in his childhood to escape from the NAZI persecution. He majored in mathematics in NYU and later gained a degree of bachelor and masters in mathematics in MIT. He then became a professor in Hebrew University and exchange professor in many world's privileged universities such as Princeton, Yale and Stanford.

He is master of game theory. Game theory was first introduced by John von Neumann and Oskar Morgenstern in 1944. With the birth of Nash Equilibrium, Game theory is analysis connected to Nash Equilibrium. However one of constantly proposed problems is the interpretation of mixed strategies, which is the basis for existence of Nash Equilibrium. The argument is that there is a mix of strategies that brings up good

▲ Professor Aumann and his wife having dinner at the 1st KIBF.

results in every competitor instead of Nash Equilibrium that is based on rationalism of individual's tendency. (Nash Equilibrium is a theory of an assembly of best strategies where the strategy is given to competitor, every attendant chooses the best strategy for themselves which will result in best balance)

In his thesis, announced in 1959, "Acceptable points in general cooperative n-person games", he provided perfect mathematical analysis for long term cooperation relations. Whether it is in the context of economy, competition or cooperation, it is an analysis based on a permanent relation base rather than a temporary relation.

Generally accepted principle of long term relation is that there will be incentives for cooperation to offset the benefits of leaving a one-time relationship. This theory is known as fork theorems which Robert J.

▲ Robert Aumann giving a lecture at the 1st KIBF.

Aumann defined it with his mathematical analysis that perfectly explains fork theorems.

In conclusion, he uplifted our understanding about conflict and cooperation through analysis of game theory. After listening to his speech, I felt that he presents difficult and complex topic as a simple and concise matter. His immeasurable depth in his study cannot be challenged as displayed in his excellent communication skills to others.

Game theory in short is a mathematical theory that analyses competitors' management abilities and chooses one's own rational plan in order to effectively achieves one's goal. Especially through 'infinitely repeated games', Aumann is the first economic scholar who analyzed people's actions in real world. He is also the first scholar ever to discover how to promote cooperation through game theory in the real world setting.

▲ At the 1st KIBF, Yoon Jong-rok, former Vice Minister of the Ministry of Science, ICT and Future Planning, former Prime Minister Ehud Olmert, and Noh Si-cheong, former Chairman of Feelux, Professor Robert Aumann.

:Israeli startup and success secrets of Israelis

He summarised secrets of Israeli startup's sucess into a few points. First secret is learning 'torah portion'. All Israelis grow up studying Torah upto a point that they can memorize it. Through Torah portion study, they remember the history of how Israel survived invasions and pressure from other strong empires and struggles they endured . Also studying torah keeps reminding them how to live as Elohim's chosen people and how to overcome the pains and scars of the past. Through Torah portion studies, they are constantly reminded of the divine history and memorize it.

Second secret to Israeli startup's success is 'hardship'. There was no proper education when Israel was in desolate and deficient environments. Israelis only harvested global success through long history of hardship. And through this hardship, they truly learned to create something out of nothing. To be successful in such deficient environment is only through efforts and training.

The third secret to success is excellent standards of work ethics. These work ethics standards are based in Torah teachings in Deuteronomy 25:13-15. Israelis apply same opportunities and principles to everyone fairly and not abandon trust between people despite of all unpredictable situations.

In order to grow together, the most important thing is not to be biased. In the law enforcement, there is always consideration for a minority. Major population can easily take away the rights of the minority. Fair distribution of opportunity and application of principles are significant. Weather a business is small or big, business cannot be sustained business without work ethics standards.

Other secrets to Israeli startup's success include government's investment policies, bald leadership of ventures, fair opportunity distribution and Hutzpha spirit. If you are an Israeli citizen, you can be given government support just like everyone else. This is because Israeli government does not make biased policies nor create economic ecosystem that are beneficial for powerful corporations.

I met professor Robert J. Aumann recently at his office in Hebrew University. He welcomed me with a clear saying;

> "Hey David, Don't forget What we have discussed before"
> "I only give others what they want to gain what I want."

In negotiation, there are always different perspectives. Then how are we to solve possible conflicts as a result of different perspectives? In the intersection of two roads, it is utmost important to make a wise decision. This is the beginning of incentives in terms of game theory. After lunch, there was a bottle of whisky on his table. As he was pouring one glass of whisky, he taught me some lessons as the master of game theory. Through the meeting with him, I realized once again why Israelis are so excellent and brilliant. I hope Koreans become close to Israeli to learn their wisdom and network.

Vice President of Check Point, Dorit Dor

One cannot talk about Israeli startup without Check Point. Because one of future strategic global businesses is 'cyber security'. Israel is world's top pioneer in cyber security industry. Because 7 million of Israel has to dwell amongst 1.3 billion Arabians, who are against them. Therefore cyber security is one of proud industries that Israel is excellent at.

South Korea also is in war with North Korea. North Korea is also a public enemy to many other countries but ironically North Korea is also a nation of the same ethnicity of South Korea that we want to unite in democracy. I am curious about the world after South and North Korea are united. For

▲ With Vice President Dorit Dor of Check Point.

this reason, cyber security is one of priorities that South Korea needs to advance in. Especially, not only for the unite with North Korea, but after the unification, Korea has to protect its nation from China and Japan, which makes cyber security even more significant to Korea.

As a benchmark model for Korea's cyber security industry, I researched about Check Point. In Israel, a startup is not founded between colleagues met in universities, work or social gatherings but a startup team is formed in military. In Israel, a startup is founded between colleagues who met in military who shared survival experiences that form a strong bond of trust.

Check Point was founded by Gill Shwed in 1993. As I emphasized before, even a startup has only one person, who is a founder, she targets global market from the beginning. They launch their homepage in English. A small company that was founded in 1993, is now a global multinational cyber security company. It is the first company that has developed network

▲ At the 3rd KIBF, with Noh Si-cheong, former chairman of Feelux, Choi Jin-seong, chairman of the board (former executive director of SKT), and Dorit Dor, vice president.

security technology in IT cyber security industry, which is now used worldwide.

Now Check Point is a global top cyber security company. Top 100 companies in USA all use cyber security solution by Check Point. Check Point is a pioneer and number one in cyber security business. Check Point consistently innovated technology based on customer oriented technology and provides wide and innovative cyber security solution to their customers.

The vice president of Check Point, Dorit is a female leader who has super power and stamina. She looked like a female warrior when she was giving a speech at the Korea and Israel Business Forum. She has a strong drive, which is what it takes to be number one. From her acquaintances, I heard how influential she was.

There is a well-known episode of hers. When she was pregnant, she took her

▲ At the 3rd KIBF with Vice President Dorit Dor and Lee Si-won, CEO of Siwon English School.

laptop in the delivery room and only when she was about to give birth in the delivery room, she could let her go of her laptop. When I met her, I wanted to ask if the above episode was really true and she confirmed that it was.

Dorit Dor is the most trusted board member by CEO Gill Shwed in Check Point. Secretaries who accompanied him endlessly complemented her. She is an irreplaceable leader in Check Point. As I was engaging in a conversation with her, I learned that she is a female leader who is bigger than life.

In Korea, we need to found a global cyber security company. If not, we at least need to give the position to companies that have cyber security capacity like Check Point. I enthusiastically encourage Korea's youngsters to specialize in cyber security area. Because if Korea does not invest in leaders in cyber security, our place might be owned by foreigners.

There is something that we are to consider in founding a startup.

> "Why should we do this?"
> "Am I the only person who can do this?"

You need to answer the above questions before starting a startup. Again, I would like to strongly appeal to Korea's young startup founders to become specialists in cyber security.

CHAPTER 03

KKUMER story

KKUMER
questions

✡

Former president of USA, Obama visited Seoul for G20. After his speech, he offered QnA time for news reporters in South Korea. Obama used to complement Korea's exceptional excellence in education to USA citizens at his early presidency. Obama indulged in cultures and current situations of Korea during his visit in Seoul. However he failed to notice one thing about Korea.

He must have thought many passionate Korean immigrants in USA achieved the 'American Dream' because of Korea's enthusiasm for education. Actually, the type of Koreans Obama have encountered in the States would

▲ Former President Barack Obama (source: EBS Documentary Prime, 'Why Do We Go to College').

have been people who are Koreans outwardly but Americans inside. His expectation to meet American Koreans in Korea was not met as there was no voluntary reporter to ask him a question in QnA time so he had to pick one Korean reporter.

However there was only silence. A few moments of awkwardness, still no reporter in Korea asked a question to Obama. The air of the room grew colder so Obama had to offer another chance to ask him a question. He even offered the help of translator this time, guessing it was the language barrier that they could not question. However there were still no questions that followed. Between a few time lapses, a Chinese CCTV reporter, Rui Chenggang, asked him a question in fluent English.

However Obama politely turned down his question and said he wanted to give Korean reporters priority and offered another chance. Obama almost pleaded Korean reporters to ask him a question for three times but still no

▲ CCTV reporter of China (source: EBS Documentary Prime, 'Why do we go to college').

Korean reporter volunteered. Inevitably, the question chance was taken by the Chinese reporter, Rui Chenggang.

How embarrassing and shameful is this incident? Obama who used to complement Korea's education, no longer mentioned it after this incident. Why? Obama could read Korea's Education problems from this incident. Did he realize that there was a limit to Korea's machine-like repetition education system? Obama perhaps realized his expectations for Korean nation's dynamics were only found in a few elite group.

Have you ever asked a question in school? Have you ever complained about social injustice? We as Koreans are used to education of uniformity like a factory manufacturing goods. When somebody raises a question and has leading thoughts, teachers get irritated. They scorn at students who ask questions in public. So, Korean students do not know how to question to authoritative figures.

Koreans get scrutinized by a society when they raise any questions. So they are afraid of questioning since childhood. If one acts that catches attention by others or have unique characteristics, it is not a good news for parents. Korean parents are not fond of the idea that their children are different from the crowd in a fear that they will not have regular or stable life.

A nation without questions. A society without questions. An individual without questions. What would have happend if we had anyone who could raise questions in Park Geun-hye administration? There is nothing more dreadful to live as a Korean citizen than this social norm of not being able to question. From global perspective, I am utterly embarrassed by Korean's current situation. Let's have questions when we live. If we are curious, we need to raise questions instead of relying on others or following the crowd.

I have to exist first before helping others to exist. If I cannot stand on my own, how can I live with others in harmony? My existence starts with questions. If I cannot question myself, I have to live a life with disguise on. If anyone is a dreamer, it has to start from a question.

KKUMERS! Let's question!

KKUMER
acts

22nd of July 2015, the due day was come.

Our prayer group of 70 youngsters prayed together to find out whether this land was given by Elohim or not and we all got the same answer that it was. We had our prayer answered that it was a land assigned by the Creator for young dreamers.

These youngsters also made donations as much as they could afford. They donated small sums of their pocket money of $100, $200, all in the gratitude to build the dream center for the next generation. In total, we

▲ Hapjeong-dong KKUMER Space contract day.

had raised 5.4 million KRW.

However we needed 50 million KRW deposit to close the real estate contract. And as time was passing, all I had was only 6.4 million KRW in my balance. I needed another 43.6 million KRW however this large sum of money could not be raised anytime soon. So I prayed to Elohim. If it is His will to build startup center for the next generation, then send me the help.

That same day, I had a lunch meeting with one of CEOs I have known for years. I escorted him to the estate in Hapjeong, sharing the story of the prayer group. At the end of the story, he offered to lend me 50 million KRW. When I look back this incident, miraculous things started happening since then. Until I was able to pay the last balance in 31st December 2015, many miraculous help was provided in a way that I could not expect.

I was without a penny when I prayed in front of the parking lot at Hapjeong real estate but I could soon manage to pay the deposit and ended up repairing the site. When I closed the property contract, the real estate agency already had a candidate before me. Also, when I made a telephone call to the real estate agent another time, one more candidate has already paid the deposit before anyone who were also on the waiting list.

I was only the third candidate and seemed like I would have no chance. However the first candidate gave up his deposit to withdraw from the contract and another candidate who was on the waiting list also gave up the property. Miraculously, the chance came to me and I could close the contract.

There is a Korean idiom, "ability is 3 and luck is 7". If I didn't believe in Elohim, it would be an ideal expression for my situation. However I believe this opportunity was given to me from Elohim. From finding this property to closing the deal, it was only through Elohim who assigned the site for the next generation of Korea as a dreaming center.

Let's have a vision. A vision that benefits others. There are two types of love in Christianity; Love Elohim and love neighbors. If those who dwell with me are happy, isn't it beneficial for all? I do not believe that everyone in this world could be happy. Even those who are wealthy and famous can have a tragic life.

However I want to believe the world I know and experience is beautiful. It is a meaningful and joyous work to give a vision and hope to someone. It is more valuable and happier life if one can move others by touching their hearts rather than a visible and tangible success.

So I am still dreaming at Hapjeong. Today, the weather is great so I was sitting at dream terrace of Hapjeong all day. I am alive with alive dream there; a dream to become a beautiful hope for the next generation. Today, I shout to others to dare to dream. I will be pumping dreams in young generation. Oh! What a wonderful day!

KKUMER
pays the price

The summer of 2015 was unbelievably hot. Under burning sun, I was remodeling the property, wiping the sweat in my forehead that was pouring like rain. When I google the property Hapjeong 376-34, the google map still shows the old site. When I compare the old site to today's building, today's KKUMER center of Hapjeong changed drastically.

Some people asked me a question. "Why are you remodeling the building that's not even yours?" I responded to them, saying "A dream center for

▲ Building appearance after remodeling in Hapjeong-dong.

the next generation should not be an ordinary space like any other space, constructed by anyone"

Of course, I am not the only one to make all changes. Firstly, it was a humble beginning by young employees who donated a seed money that I was able to close the property contract. Those who could not aid financially, came and labored to reconstruct the building such as gardening and painting. When a change is made by a single person, the change is owned by one single person.

However, when people dream together and march together, it has a great power of dynamics. However it's still not enough. Because a new history is not made by one hero. It requires many supporting roles and extras who walk together to write a new history. However many leaders forget the team work and hurry.

An excellent leader does not work alone. He does not insist that he is the only one who right. He suggests a vision to drive a group to walk towards the vision with a great ability. However there is always noise and confusion along the way. A leader can be subjected to enormous criticism and even loud arguments. When I was building a hardware of Hapjeong KKUMER center, I came to think the importance of this process.

However, I had to pay various price, which was unexpected. We had different views by each individual in the community. I had to decide. I politely warned those to withdraw from this project if they had a different vision and I had to go through a pain as 50% of the members quit. When

▲ Hapjeong-dong KKUMER Space Remodeling Project.

I reflect this incident, it was my fault.

However, the most important thing to walk in a vision in the future is to pay the price for it. Even if it takes pain and hardship, one has to endure. Because not everyone could have one mind and not everyone could be correct. When I look back, I sometimes regret and it was a very lonely time. However it is impossible to accomplish a dream without price.

Instead, it is very significant to learn lessons from failure. One has to embed such hard learned lessons and try one's best to not to make the same mistakes. I myself cannot forget these lessons. When I reflect the failures, I admit that it was all my fault. I do not blames others but I blame it on myself. So I want to tell this to young generation who persist their dreams.

"You need to pay price for your vision."

Especially, lessons from failures tend to repeat. It is important to record the mistake to reflect in order not to repeat the same mistakes. Today, I want to encourage those who ride on the dream race.

KKUMER
grows through failures

On 22nd July 2015, I finally made it to KKUMER center, Hapjeong. After first remodeling of the building, we had a modest open party. Everyone celebrated impressed. However all team members were worried and burdened at the same time. Because they were worried that the scale of the hardware is too large in comparison to the typical work style of mine.

It was not the climate of the nature of the work they were worried about. It took ten months to officially open KKUMER center from 22nd July

▲ Hapjeong-dong KKUMER Space's initial building.

2015 to 30th May 2016. I had changed the front sign for three times and endured rough times. I had to spend everyday batting my life to accomplish KKUMER vision in reality.

The first front sign read 'KAIC Global Startup Center', which got many pedestrians wondering. The building looked broke as it had no proper maintenance for the last ten years. It had burst of leafy trees and the interior of the building was from 35 years ago. Everything had to be renovated; electricity, paint, water, sewage and waterproof.

Old buildings are usually not capable of insulation and waterproof so our summer and winter were miserable. The amount of electricity was inadequate to supply the power to the whole building. Everything needed renovation in another words extra money. All I had was donation from the people and 6 thousand KRW from cafe deposit.

Since then, I literally labored. I designed the architecture and labored with labour workers. I was a stranger to architecture. I was born into a prosperous family and had no experiences in extreme labour. When I was a teenager, only wealthy people could go study abroad. I was so called 'gold spooner'

However I went through a harsh labour for the first time in my life. From a mentor of young CEOs, I became a labour man with soil and sweat. So I started studying about architecture. When I had questions, I asked expert architects to continue renovating the site. And many worries of people became true.

In architecture, one has to see the whole forest before trees. If one sees only trees instead of forest, he keeps making the same mistakes. After repairing, there are another spots to be repaired, which ends up in repetitive pattern of repairing the same matter again. After this ridiculously repetitive pattern of renovation, I grew extremely disappointed and exhausted. So I developed a habit of inquiring to expert architects before I make any commitments.

After renovation of KAIC Global Startup Center at KKUMER Center, I changed the front sign for the second time. It was a bald claim that reflect my strong will and challenge. "Startup fearlessly". After this front sign stood up, many residents came and asked what this space was about. Hapjeong-dong is an old village and it had many generational residents.

They were unfamiliar with startup incubating facility so the building became the talk of the town. They knew well about the building as it had the size of the building was 300 pyeong(about 990m^2) with giant tree surroundings. However they were astonished at how renovation changed its appearance with new buildings inside.

One of them came and asked me if I was a famous architect. They were used to seeing old and runout building instead of seeing this new building of landmark. Second front sign became a good tool to introduce 'startup business' to residents of Hapjeong-Dong.

I also demolished all pillars except only three of them. I thought new wine needed to held at a new wineskin which led to a bald demolition. When I demolished the doors and opened the garden, residents of Hapjeong-Dong loved the idea. Everyone was mysterious about the building but now they could see beautiful flowers and trees in the open.

The reason why I left the three pillars to remain is to mix traditional appearance and modern image of innovation to co-exist. However after I built the building, the clash of iron and stone did not go harmoniously. So I made another big decision to demolish the three pillars that used to be the symbol of the building. From this day on, I could not go home.

Because we were not free from outside invasion as the gates of the building were wide open. I labored in the morning and stood for surveillance at night, I ran out of all my energy. However I did not feel such every level but had inexplainable power to carry on. I was happy to see how KKUMER Center transforms on daily base.

After completion of KKUMER Center, I went through numerous failures. I often regret learning lessons a hard way. I had a lot of pressure for I had to renovate and build from a limited budget. I learned something from extreme hardship. KKUMER grows from failures. KKUMER can fail but never give up. KKUMER does not make the same mistake.

A dreamer likes to learn from failures. Because the process of accomplishing dreams does not come at no cost. Lessons learned from various failures are imprinted in his heart and does the best at the next go. I have learned to establish my dreams stronger from failures. KKUMERS, do not be afraid of failures.

KKUMER
fixes kennel twelve times

If you have a dog, you have got to get a dog a dog house. Generally, people would buy a dog house or build a dog house for once. Even a dog lover would concede these extraordinary efforts to build their own dog house. However my thoughts are different. If I was to have a dog, how many times would I build a dog house?

If I had a dog, I would build a dog house for twelve times a year. Because after I make a dog house, I would find out shortcomings to supplement. It will be the same time after time. I would build a dog a better house to be better and stronger over and over.

Not even twelve times, but I would constantly develop the dog house as long as I live. Because I find happiness and worth in making

changes, acting, creating and bringing life to something. After constant development of a dog house will allow me to discover new findings and terrific value and philosophy.

As a person ages, he usually would like to settle down for a sense of stability. It is a natural thing as life gets more and more dramatic. As I become over 50, I personally hope my life to get less dramatic. Perhaps,

I have come to a realization how hard it is to live for others especially when I am not as capable nor influential.

I think I would fix a dog house until I die. Firstly, I have a pioneer DNA and I have acquired a taste for endless change but I also believe I have a historical mission for this ever changing time. I believe. A person who fixes a dog house twelve times is more future forward and independent than a person who builds a dog house for one time.

Now it's a generation of 100. Generally people retire at their 60s or 70s. What would a person do for the rest of 30 to 40 years? Usually, people age rapidly after retirement. Because they suddenly have a lot of time at hand after their repetitive work hours. Especially, salary men who are used to receive wages feel burdened to turn from passive life to active life to manage extra hours.

▲ KKUMER is a person who constantly fixes the doghouse by himself.

However, a person who fixes a dog house for twelve hours has a pioneer spirit to overcome any situations and difficulties. A person who fixes a dog house to constantly develop, is a person who can pioneer new career after retirement.

There is no retirement in my life. There is rest and restoration but no retirement. Retiring is death. So I fix the dog house today. It is not only young people's right to endlessly try and rise from failures, but it is the right for those who live their life actively. I want to encourage young generation to rise again and finish building the dog house.

KKUMER rises from despair

Hapjeong-dong 376-34⋯.
Seongji road 40⋯.

When I look at my registration of address that lists old address and new address, it gives me a little laughter. When I first made it to Hapjeong-dong, the old address appeared however after renovation, a new address appeared. Many people ask me the same question over and over; what is my secret to build the KKUMER center for the next generation on such a vast land and with newly constructed buildings?

▲ Hapjeong-dong KKUMER Space Entrepreneurship Slogan.

However I want to point out that people tend to judge based on hardware. Success is measured by one's accomplishments. However I want to say that visibility and tangibility are not everything in assessing success. What's more important than visible and tangible success is a success often hidden and invisible and one has to experience it to really understand the invisible success. What is a definition of success? Is it success only it has a visible accomplishment?

I define success as a verb instead of a noun. The dictionary definition of success is to accomplish one's goal(s). Therefore I interpret success as an ongoing action instead of a noun. Those who say that I am successful have an incredible insight in them. They see the essence in me that is not replicable. However many young generation tries to merely copy me.

Do you know despair? What is despair? It means a situation that has no hope. What many successful people have in common is that they rise up again from despair. How could one start again from failure? As I lived my life, I realized that one has to fail in order to succeed. Success without failure is like building a house on sand.

When I reflect my life, I could rise up again because of my failures. I was a successful business man when I was 20 and unafraid of anything. I succeeded in every business I did and knew no failures. However I spent an extremely hard time in IMF for one year of my life. After this hardship, life was renewed again. It was the first time that I realized what it is like to fail in life. It was the time of desperation that I don't even want to look back.

I realized one thing back then. All relationships I have when I thrive, are meaningless. True relationships are those who stayed besides me when I was at my rock bottom. Who are the people that understand, cherish and love me the most? I still do not trust people because you do not know people's true colors until they hit their rock bottom.

So I like people who have failed before than those are successful. I prefer meeting with those who are overcoming failures than those who are successful. Because there is always a crowd forming surrounding successful people. And often they mistake these crowd people as their true friends. However once the bubble goes away, a crowd of people vanishes.

People are usually interested in the network I have. Korean people always look for connections when they initiate business. "Do you know somebody? Can you connect me to this person?" Because they need these connections in order to accomplish what they are about to do. However this type of people always fail for 100%. It is like building a house upon the sand to rely one's business based on relationships and connections instead of one's authentic ability and efforts.

As I lived good years of my life, it is not a true success if one does not succeed in the following. If one does not have a sustainable growth and innovation, success will always flee from him. Success is like a bonus to those who constantly make efforts and pay the price. Because success does not settle next to you but it always has its way to flee from you and you have to make efforts to chase after and grasp upon it.

One has to have a desperation. The desperation I am talking about is life worth efforts that come after failures. Have you spent sleepless nights? Have you ever faced crisis that seems like there is no way out in these sleepless nights? I still have these sleepless nights. It is my daily routine.

Especially when I first built KKUMER center, I despaired everyday of my life. Still, there are people who are questioning me about the hardware. How I was able to afford to build new buildings at such a large property. They assume I was funded by many wealthy men around me. However I literally despaired everyday of my life to build this KKUMER center.

I spent sleepless nights worrying about the wages I had to pay for construction laborers. I also had many negative doubts weather I could actually finish the construction and have a proper opening. Within this one year period of construction, I had suicidal thoughts to commit suicide at the balcony with a rope. I really thought my life would end there.

Many people left me and some betrayed me. Many rumors were forming about me. Many seniors and adults who have known me for years came to comfort me with deep concern, saying;

> "I trust you David, you always rose up again from many life's storms that inspired others. Same will happen again this time."

One year of fighting endless despair, I built KKUMER center. I was a best friend with failure, whom I also fought everyday. I also discovered new hopes sprout from difficulties and sighs. I am still a good friend with despair.

▲ With Noh Si-cheong, former chairman of Feelux, Son Hye-won, former member of the National Assembly, and Choi Jin-seong, former executive director of SKT (from right).

It is a good motivation to train me. Its another name is hope as hardship sustains me.

30th May 2016, KKUMER center had its hard earned opening celebration. Many came to celebrate the opening of the KKUMER center. VIPs such as Mayor Hongseop Park of Mapo-gu, Politician Hyewon Son, CEO Sicheong Noh, of Feelux, Jinseong Choi of SK Telecom CTO came and gave opening speeches. Suddenly a lot of crowd formed. I could take a photo of me smiling for the first time in a long time.

However I still despair to this day. When will the day of stability come? Ironically, I do not believe there is such day as a stable day. Even if it comes, I think I will still befriend with despair. However I am building KKUMER center though these hardships. Despair is not a very good friend. But surely it is a good soil for success.

I despair today. I sometimes beat it and sometimes lose. When can I end this battle? However I have come to a deep realization of its lessons. I always live my life with the lessons imprinted in my heart. I speak to many of young generation. A story of hope to rise from despair to those who don't know it.

No one likes despair. However it is a bitter medicine for those race towards success. So I always tell my story of failures to those who visit me. True success is a success that overcame deepest failures. Through KKUMER center, I witness true success that overcame despair.

▲ Hapjeong-dong KKUMER Space Opening Event.

KKUMER
leads the future

27th January 2011, a group of 33 young CEOs gathered in Kensington Hotel Yeouido Seoul. I organized a group of young CEOs called '*enfant terrible*'. The intention was simple. I was a successful business man in my 20s and 30s. I went through hard storms in my 30s to 40s and met my turning point. Since then, I decided to become a mentor instead of a star.

My life in short, I was a fearless young man with successful business. The time when I did business was 80s and 90s when Korea was radically developing and many businesses prospered. As I had a lot of wealth and

▲ CEO MBA Vision Impact Meeting.

fame, I was busy indulging in them. A half time came in my 40s after seamless ride of my young self.

I observed many young successful CEOs like I once was. There was one common thing in these young CEOs had in common. It was a question of fear and unpredictability of their business's future. "How far can I sustain my business success?" I also had the same question when I was a young entrepreneur.

So I founded a magazine called 'Christian CEO'. Because I am a Christian, I called out young CEOs who dream to achieve honest and clean wealth. Those young successful CEOs agreed at my statement. They were interested in my mentoring. I suggested to them to invite successful entrepreneurs to receive mentoring.

A group of 33 young CEOs had a monthly meeting at Kensington Hotel Yeouido Seoul hotel to learn from senior entrepreneurs who accomplished great success from soil. It became a foundation for the establishment of 'KOREA ISRAEL BUSINESS COUNCIL'. However it did not excel from the beginning. All business men tend to test something. It could be expressed as cautious or hesitant.

However I did not try to accomplish something over night. If I got the young CEOs the help they needed through mentoring, I thought I did everything I could. Essentially it gave birth to today's committee members. When I look back, it was a miraculous event. It only took 3 weeks to gather 33 CEOs who wanted to participate in my vision and philosophy.

This group started off from members of promising young entrepreneurs of 20s and 30s who are full of energy such as; CEO Siwon,Lee of Siwon English School, CEO Hyunwoo, Park of InnoRed, CEO Jongsuk,Kim of Hello Kitty, CEO Dongjin Lee of Coffee of Dream, CEO Youngseo, Lim of Porridge Story and Attorney Myeongseop Kim of RootsAlae Law Firm After, CEOs of listed companies and medium sized business joined the committee. CEO Seonyong LEE from TGIF Korea served as a senior for the committee.

Now they all have become CEOs of prosperous and renown companies. They are all renowned figures in the business sector they are in. They have become skillful entrepreneurs in their ability and business outcomes. How have they achieved such success? I believe it is because these young CEOs have a good character and personality.

Not all of them are Christians but most of them are Christians. In Christianity, we are to love neighbors like we love God and serve the world as the light and salt of the world. We have a servanthood to serve for bigger cause instead of my own benefits. They also endured many difficulties in business through faith.

From now on, I want to talk about how dreamers accomplish their dreams based on their past and present. First of all, they did not climb where they are by gazing upon the sky. They made endless efforts and endured hard times to be where they are now and now can confidently witness to their juniors.

"No Cross, No Crown."

Investing in Global Entrepreneurs and Enterprises

Now I have become 50s and living the second half of my life. As I was reflecting my life, many things have happened. The most remarkable experience in my life would be to encounter Israel. Growing under prestige parents, I was able to study abroad in the USA and had a prolific business at young age. However my life was not global until I met Israel.

However as I have come to know Israel, I truly learned what global meant because I have come to meet VIPs of Israel's global leaders. I do not have a big existence in Korea. I am just one of ordinary citizens. However when I

▲ Korea's startup legend Byun Dae-gyu, chairman, with Israel's startup legend Dove Moran.

visit Israel, I am treated like a Korean ambassador from Israelis.

I communicate with VIPs of Israel's global leaders through emails and in person. However I do not know the chair of Seoul university. Actually it would be like getting blood out of stone for me to meet him. Even if I try, I do not know connections to meet him. If I wanted to email him, I would not be able to as I don't know his email address but even if I did and sent him an email, my attempts will be filtered from the management level.

However I am able to communicate with Israel's global leaders such as chairs of universities, Nobel prize winners, CEOs of global companies at any time. I can call them directly to organize meetings. It does not have to go through middle person such as secretaries or board members but I can directly call and email to make an appointment. This is the difference between Korea and Israel.

One time, a legendary Israeli entrepreneur, an inventor of USB, Dov Moran made a visit to Korea. I gave him a tour guide in his visit. I appointed a meeting with CEO of a legendary startup HUMAX, Daegyu Byun and held a meeting together. After this meeting, Dov told me to go to Samsung. Later, I found out he meant the vice president of Samsung, Lee Jae-yong

I have never met vice president of Samsung, Lee Jae-yong. If it was in Israel, I would easily visit Samsung to meet vice president of Samsung, Lee Jae-yong. Unfortunately, Korea still has vain formalities and authorities. Those who were born into entitled positions would not meet people out of their league. However I can meet much more successful and famous global leaders of Israel than vice president of Samsung, Lee Jae- yong.

Do we have Nobel prize winners in Korea? Technion university of technology has brought seven Nobel prize winners. I can meet the chair of Technion university whenever. This is a global network. Why was Korea not able to grow Nobel prize winners? Because Korea is not a global country. If a nation is not global, it means it is a boiling frog. The great walls of a big company have now fallen. However Korea is still considered republic of Samsung.

There is a national equation that says if Samsung falls, Korea falls too. Of course, it will have a huge damage. However it is such a silly nationalism and nonsensical lie if Korea falls when Samsung falls. I guarantee Korea will not fall even if Samsung does. If Korea falls because of Samsung, it's not even a country.

▲ Along with Dove Moran and Ryu Joong-hee, CEO of Future Play, who M&A his startup to Intel.

There was a global M&A. Global American company Intel bought a small Israeli startup for astronomical amount at 17.56 trillion. Can you imagine? This amount of money can easily merge and acquisition an average America's global company. Israel's startup exits their company at this scale of money.

In fact, there are numerous Israeli startups that sell startups at hundreds and hundreds million dollars from America's giant cooperations. This is not a rare event at all. Sometimes at trillion dollars even. When Israel founds a startup, they target global. Even if there is only one founder, Israel makes English homepage first.

The strength of Israel's startup comes from global. Even it's one founder's startup, they knock on the global market. A nation of population of 7 million invest in global leaders and grow together. USA is a tabloid edition of Israel. The son in law of the former USA president Trump is Jewish. He is not just the son in law but he is a senior adviser of the White House.

America is a mere cover. The content of America is all created by Jewish brains. I call this the power of Jewish network. Everyone knows a nation of 7 million population is the engine of world's most powerful country America. However only Korea is willingly rejects this fact. Actually they do not know how to approach this fact.

There is a Korean idiom "you have to hang out with rich men to be a rich man". You have to socialize with rich people in order to learn basic techniques such as ideas, habits, ways to learn money, network and etc. I dare to guarantee if one needs go global, you need to know Israeli network. You need to think, act, and play like Israelis.

Creation starts from copying. If you copy hard enough, you will be eventually able to paint your own picture and creation will be your ability. In order for Koreans to empower global leaders and startups, we need to learn from Israel, but not on a surface level but through networking with global Israelis by having decent conversations and building relationships. So far, I have learned what it means to be global from Israeli leadership.

I have come to a conclusion from seeing Israeli global leaders that if Korea does not go global, it will not survive. Korea is trapped between China and Japan and USA puts pressure upon Korea for its own national benefits. How can Korea survive in the conflicting situation from its surrounding powerful countries? The only answer is we need to grow global leaders and startups.

After I discover the world of Israel, I witnessed how Israel invests in global leaders and startups with my own eyes. I took Korean leaders to Israel and got them educated under Israel's global startup incubation system paying with my own money. I took Korea's startup leaders and got them to do IR before Israel's global VCs. One of them was CEO of DOT, Eric Kim.

Korea is at its crisis. If we do not innovate now, we will follow the steps of South American countries. Once prosperous countries like Argentina had to go through shameful time. The only way for Koreans to survive is to invest in global leaders and startups. Korea as a nation has to pour all our energy to discover global leaders and investing in them. If our government does not do it, I will.

There is a phrase that meets the eye of visitors first at KKUMER center. It's written in English. Why is it in English? I wrote it in English because we need to global.

"HERE COMES THAT DREAMER."

This slogan of KKUMER center is not what I came up with. It is a word of God in genesis. Before Joseph becoming Israel's leader to redeem the nation, he was persecuted by his own brothers. This is what his brothers mocked Joseph with "HERE COMES THAT DREAMER".

However exactly 30 years later, Joseph's brothers had kneel down before Joseph begging for their lives. Joseph forgave his brothers. The point is that dreamers usually get mocked and humiliated. However the world is dreamers' stage.

Dreamers dream globally and live globally to accomplish their global dreams. Let's have dreams but have global dreams. Korea is a small stage compare to global stage. Now you can rule the world with a computer on desk. To become a global entrepreneur, young generation has to pay the price it needs.

I still believe there is hope in Korea. However there is no hope if Korea doesn't go global. Therefore I want to pass on my know-how to Korea's next young generation. However the resource is restricted hence the advantage goes to a restricted number. If you read this book and have a global dream, I want to invite you to Hapjeong. I want to have your back.

The London Eye of Seoul in Hapjeong

I want to make a Ferris wheel on the valley, overlooking Han-river at Hapjeong to attract tourists from all around the world like London Eye in UK. I went to Gyeongseong High School' at Yeonnam-dong nearby Hapjeong. This town is now called 'Yeontral Park' where the retro train road brings nostalgia of the time of president Chun Doo-hwan. There were many armed policemen and many protestors of democracy. I went to high school for two years there. I still have memories playing with my friends at this train road when I was first grade at high school.

Yeonnam-dong, Hongik university, Hapjeong-dong are places of my high school memories. Now I do business in the same town in 2015. This town is where biggest crowd of young generation forms. Millions of young generation goes to work, shopping and entertain. I built a startup hub in this town for the young generation. I wanted to bridge the gap between senior and junior generations and I built KKUMER Space, centering around the young generation in 2015. When I made the KKUMER playground, it was not built from my own possession. Entrepreneurs with like minded and a group of young generation raised donations and I myself also invested all my possession into it.

As KKUMER Space was becoming a stable establishment, Kim Mi-Sook head of Hapjeong District suggested a proposal. She said she wanted to participate in this meaningful cause so we ended up building KKUMER BUILDING at her real estate, another startup incubation center was born. I managed architecture by myself for both properties at Hapjeong. After finishing these two buildings, construction works are extremely hard. I had to initiate the building project at an expert level from planning, building bases, electricity, facilitation and negotiating with veteran construction workers. This process was obviously not easy. However I had persistently pursued to complete the construction, overcoming a few conflicts with the construction workers along the way.

After completion of the construction at Hapjeong, I was give an offer from Gyeonggi Business & Science Accelerator at Pankyo. It was a global startup accelerator project to promote Korea's startups to launch abroad. Accelerators were TechStar of USA, Xinova and SOSA of Israel. They offered me to launch SOSA of Israel in Korea to operate a global accelerator project. Therefore I spent the year of 2019 to launch Israel's global accelerator, SOSA to promote Korea's startups to go global. There is no easy task in life. I understand Israel's tactics of persistence and shameless attitude. After one year of painfully time consuming business negotiations, I have learned important lessons.

After going through many unpredictable events, I held an opening of Startup Campus at Pankyo on 15th January 2020. Many VIPs including Han Jeong-hwa of Ministry of SMEs and Startups from Park Geun-hye administration came to celebrate the accomplishment. When Minister Han Jeong-hwa was in the position, I served as a general secretary at

Korea Israel Business Council, promoting startup economy of Israel in Korea. Six years after, I asked the former Han Jeong-hwa Ministry of SMEs and Startups to give a opening speech at SOSA Korea, a partnership between Korea and Israel businesses. It was a dream come true moment of Korea and Israel's official startup collaboration after almost ten years time period of knocking on the door of Israel. Even though the process was painstakingly slow, a good outcome came after constant efforts.

However as soon as SOSA opened, Covid19 broke out. The whole world was locked down in the pandemic. I expected it to last six months however variants of the virus had kept occurring and left the world terrified. It was the worst nightmare that no one saw it coming. There was nothing I could do in this lockdown. I could not progress much work because the world was put on a stop. I could not come up with a solid breakthrough. Instead, I thought and examined various works for the next generation as always. Because the next generation will live in a fast changing and open world unlike my generation.

And I also was able to build another KKUMER zone called KKUMER Playground at Hapjeong-dong overlooking Han-river. It was a five story building on the hill overlooking Han-river that indulges mixed contents of all experiences at Hapjeong-dong and Pankyo. Total seven sectors of contents consists of Korea Israel Business Council, KKUMER Space, Play &, Future IT & Society (FITS), K Space, Hills Cafe and etc were complete. Until then, it was one man leadership but now all my work was segmented into independent entities that transitioned its management to juniors to co-lead the Korea and Israel dream. Now what I can do is to develop a system for juniors to stand on their own feet.

There is a major business for KKUMER Playground at Hapjeong-dong. It is to build a great wheel at a large property of 2,000 sqft at Hapjeong-dong nearby Han-river. London eye is the ideal model for this project. This business model is already validated at London. This business model called 'London Eye' attracted 4.2 million tourists, created 1100 occupations and generated income model worth more than 35 billion won. I want to build a great wheel here. Because I want to build a cultural town for young generation on this 1400 soft property from the profit earned by the great wheel. The first story of this cultural town will install a shopping mall with diverse cuisine and sceneries to attract many youngsters like Hongdae road.

The second story of the town will be a startup hub. It will be a global startup space of Korean and Israeli creative minds. I have worked with visionaries of like minded without government and cooperation support. Would it be too impossible to build the second Silicon Valley by Korean and Israeli dream team here at Hapjeong-dong? I do not believe so. The future will be innovated by IT. IT will merge the whole wide world as one flat space. The world of IT will be centered in Korea and Israel after USA and Europe. This is not just a dream of mine but realistic vision.

Of all the countries around the world, only Korea and Israel can transform the world through innovative IT technologies. Korea and Israel are the only nations who have advanced by diasporas. The whole nation uses the automatic system of semiconductor, telecommunication and IT. Israel is surrounded by 1.3 billion Arabian countries who are against them. However Israel is fighting against 1.3 billion Arabian countries with only population of 9 million and yet Israel has never been defeated. Israel has world's most powerful army to win 13 versus 1 battle. This is the core strength of Israel that even countries of 1.3 billion population cannot take over.

South Korea is still a divided country. It is at ideology war with North Korea. Fortunately, South Korea has achieved a tremendous economic growth as a demographic country. However North Korea has become one of the poorest countries led by communist dictatorship by the three sons of Kim Il-sung. North Korea threatens the whole world with their nuclear weapon. Especially they constantly threaten South Korea to have economic supplies from South Korea. South Korea is also jammed between China and Japan. If we were not a powerful country, there would be nothing that we could do in the middle. If South Korea was not backed with economic and military power, we would just be a sandwich country between China and Japan. For this reason, South Korea needs to hold hand with Israel.

There will be endless opportunities if Korea's manufacturing strength is combined with Israel's innovative technologies in this conflicting situation suppressed by outer countries. Israel is an inventor of world's first technologies then they sell these pioneering technologies in Silicon Valley at astronomical value. It is not a made up story when we hear an Israeli startup with seed money of $2,000 was sold at 17.56 trillion by Intel USA. Israel's startups have been globalized for a long time and recocgnized throughout

USA and European countries. South Korea is to utilize this global network of Israelis and their inventive global technologies. Because simply there is no country that is capable of what Israel does. It takes decades if not centuries of work and finance to form a global economic infrastructure and organization.

How do I speak of such a daring dream? And who are with me? It could seem like a picturesque fantasy to others but there are people who are marching towards this vision with me. Because of all things I have spoken have come to reality. Every vision I have proclaimed since the year 2015 at Hapjeong-dong has become reality. At that time, everyone predicted that my plans will fail. People who were closest to me were making negative comments on what I do and grew distant from me. Now all visions I have proclaimed, have literally come to reality in the year 2022. Likewise, all proclamations made in the year 2021 will come true. There were no predictions that didn't.

Some people say that they are nervous when I initiate a new project. The average percentage that a new business to succeed is only 10% by big companies. Their question is if large multinational companies have such a small rate, how could I lead a success in new businesses? Their point is correct. A person like me who has no money and influential connections has less than 1% of success rate. However miraculously, I succeeded in everything I did and attracted adequate investment. Now there is a trust base network formed to raise adequate fund for new projects. How did I manage to thrive my business in this recession time from covid pandemic?

Because I walked persistently with my eyes set on the goals in solitude. I despised what others said but persisted in my mission for the next generation.

The young generation is aching. Why? Because they see no ladder of hope. My generation, which is often referred as 586 generation was the time of high economic growth with wide range of career opportunities. It was not as hard as now to buy a home and build a family if we tried. However today's generation has lost a ladder of hope. It costs average 1 billion KRW to buy a dwelling place in Seoul. The real estate market in Seoul is already out of league for young generation to penetrate. What can we do? It is a responsibility of 586 generation to take care of the next generation. Instead of lecturing them on how to become an adult overcoming hardships, they actually have to build a ladder of hope. Today, I dream for a hopeful future in KKUMER playground at Hapjeong-dong, Namsan, Gangnam and Pankyo.

The next Korea's Israeli Ambassador

As mentioned previously, Korea and Israel have many things in common. Both nations have gone under endless invasions from surrounding countries. Both nations are always standing at the edge of a cliff from other countries' attempts to wipe out our territories. Both nations have deficiency of natural resources, which inevitably placed the nations to advance in cutting edge technologies in order to earn sole independency. There are no future if we don't invest in the next generation for both countries. Although Korea and Israel have devastating deficiencies, there are more strengths that overcome weaknesses. It is an invincible will. Throughout continuous tormented history that Korea and Israel have gone through, both countries survive backed by military power and technology advancement. These ethnicities only grow stronger under persecution. Where does the strength come from?

The more persecution there is, the stronger the nation becomes. Why? Israel was invaded by Rome in AD72. After siege of Jerusalem, Rome decided to scatter Israelis throughout the world because of their strong nationalism, which Rome saw it as a threat. Israelis already went through wrongful destruction of their country but they were then forecefully scattered throughout the world to live as refugees. They had wandered around the world as refugees for 2,000 years. The cruel history of Israel did not end there. Palestines were immigrated to the land of Israel to deport Israelis for good. The sad tragedy of Israel's history scarred the nation forever.

The scattered Israeli diasporas can be seen all throughout all continents including Europe, USA and Asia. There is one thing that the diaspora Israelis must do despite of their refugee lifestyle. They build synagogue wherever they go and learn Hebrew language. They share traditional Israel food and educate people to not to forsake their ethnic identity. Despite of the harsh political climate, Jews prospered through their synagogues. They never forsook to educate the people of Israel of the history and culture to renew and develop as a nation. All diaspora Israelis gathered at synagogue on the appointed times and prayed for Aaliyah. (Return to Israel)

The WWII broke out and Germans attacked the Britains. As UK was being pushed to the edge, they asked for financial help from Jews for military funding. With this opportunity, Jews had negotiated with Sir Winston Leonard Spencer-Churchill of the Britain to sign a document that consents Israel as a constitution after war, in turn. The united army took the victory and the Britains kept their words with Israelis. They deported the Palestine habitants from the land of Israel to establish a nation. After 2,000 years of losing their homeland to Palestines, Israel finally got their land back.

Two ethnicities ended up living in the same land at different time period. 2,000 years ago, it was Israel's and another 2,000 years, it belonged to Palestines. Now these two ethnicities are fighting over this sacred land.

From an objective perspective, they both have rational arguments in their own rights. The reason for this paralleled conflicts goes back to their roots.

They have the same forefather but come forth from different genealogy and have been fighting like enemies. This conflict of thousands and thousands years accumulation cannot be solved easily. It would be a lie if it was solved easily. Recently, there was a face to face conversation attempt is made between these two ethnicities. I hope for the peace of Jerusalem which is a trembling cup in the Middle East. If this generational conflict could be solved through political engineering, it would greatly contribute the world peace and eliminate risks of war, like killing two birds with one stone.

There is a reason why I want to become an ambassador for Israel in South Korea. A good relation between both countries will result in advancing world economy. No country can complete with Israel's global infrastructure, remote communication and network that were built by Israeli diasporas. All first and best inventive technologies of the world economy are owned by Israel. On the other hand, Israel does not have manufacturing back up. Israel has pioneering and cutting edge technologies but these technologies are not necessarily linked to manufacturing process but are sold at a global market instead. When Israel's cutting-edge technologies and Korea's strong manufacturing base meet, it will create incredible synergy and world's best dream team. Productive cooperation of Korea and Israel will vastly contribute to world economy and ultimately prosperity of both countries.

However relation of Korea and Israel still has comparatively small political influence to bond these two nations. There was a record breaking number of trade occured in Korea and China's trad history to have 800 flights in a day between Korea and China. Korea and Israel need to boost our capacity to strengthen our relation and technology exchange. We are to build bridge that integrates politics, economy, culture and art to activate Korea Israel relation. There needs to be a long term relation between VIPs of both countries. Furthermore, political comprehension and cooperation between generals and politicians of both countries are needed. A closer network between people of Korea and Israel is needed to promote development of both countries.

In order to accomplish the above, an expert who has a thorough understanding in both countries' culture, art, history, politics and economy has to build a bridge. There is a considerable number of Korean experts of Israel religiously. Two countries have been interchanging actively based on tourism. However it will advance even further if political and economic relation advances. The combined efforts of the two nations in technology inventions by Israel and manufacturing and distribution channel by Korea will induce enormous influential potential. It does not take only one side to excel to create a great synergy. An expert who loves Israel, should tune Korea and Israel's relation to advance the partnership without agenda.

All Israelis go to army at young age. In army, they seriously get to think about life and death at young age. After army service, they go to college. In Korea, high school graduates go to college immediately but Israelis go to college after building some social experiences. So Israelis learn everything they need to learn about life in the military. Israeli military does not only teach military skills but basic lessons for life. In Israel, all genders are obliged to go to army and army is a school for important life experiences. In army, Israel's young generation learns life and plans for the future.

Israeli army is also a fervent soil for startup. Army colleagues often team up to found startups together. Israeli army is a great place to found a startup. Many military skills turn into technologies needed for innovative startups. For example, Israeli army unit, Unit820 is only dedicated to hacking tasks. There is no military or company that Unit820 cannot penetrate. The number one global cyber security company that Unit820 has brought forth is Argus. Korea's Samsung is also investing in Argus. For Israelis, military is not a place that brains regress but learn about startups and potential work colleagues.

A small nation of Israel of 9 million is leading the world. Israel has exceptional strengths and technology. However Korea is quite blind to Israel's global power just yet. In another words, Korea is still unaware of Korea and Israel's relational synergy as Israel is quite a foreign land to most of people in Korea. If I was to became an ambassador of Israel, I want to bridge between Korea and Israel in politics, economy, culture, arts and history to fundamentally build the base for the relation. I would like to contribute to Korea and Israel relation with all my expertise in Israel, using all my knowledge and network to build a strong bond ever.

I still have a vivid impression on my first visit at Israel. They welcomed a stranger like me with 'Shalom'. In this simple greeting, it reflects

Israel's unique history and culture. When you visit Jerusalem, one of the first things you will notice is 'Dome of the Rock' by Islam. This co-existence of good and evil in this sacred land, it holds a hidden treasure of mysterious truth in it. The good will towards Israel lays in the next young generation. I hope for the future where Korea and Israel's young creative minds get together to challenge the future of the world by global technology and network to write a new history and create culture.

I would like to dedicate the second half of my life to build this base for Korea and Israel's relation. I hope the network of Israel's VIP plays a role of bridgehead to bridge between the two nations. I believe it is a perfect destiny guided by Elohim. Only Elohim will open a new road of Korea and Israel's politics, economy, culture, arts and history. The synergy of the two nations will be roadmap for the world economy. I do not mind living as a door man of the two countries if it could contribute to the advancement of Korea and Israel's relation to be more influential. I live my life with my eyes set on this ultimate goal. I need to become a diplomat in order to become an ambassador of Israel.

However I cannot officially become an ambassador because I am not a government official. However there is a 'special ambassador' policy. An expert who is considered to develop the relation of Korea and Israel in terms of politics, economy, arts and culture, can be referred to become an ambassador. If I can be subjected to this privilege, I would like to dedicate the second half of my life to advance the relation of Korea and Israel. I believe it is a task that can be done by a dreamer. Even if I do not become an ambassador of Israel, it cannot stop my passion. I am a dreamer. I will live as a dreamer after 60s, chasing the dream that Elohim gave me. A dreamer is happiest when he dreams. I live my happy dream today as a bridge between Korea and Israel.

KKUMER Playground is a Vision Stage for the Next Generation

I have reflected the last ten years of journey to plan the next ten years for KKUMER Playground. I have held numerous forums and conferences between Korea and Israel through the VIP network of Israel in all social aspects including startup, economy, politics and culture. I have managed multiple projects to support and bridge investors and startup founders of both countries through various field trips to Israel and invitations to South Korea for Korea's startups and entrepreneurs to anchor their global success in Israel. As a result, I have fostered creative spaces for the next entrepreneurs and built a dream team. Now, the remaining tasks are how are we to execute KKUMER Playground's visions and values into a reality based on the last ten years of hard efforts?

First - KKUMER Playground for the next generation

Through special destiny with Israel, Korea Israel Business Council (KIBC) was founded and it took another ten years to launch KKUMER Playground. Through small successes built from numerous failures and despairs, the vision and the philosophy of KKUMER Playground could be established. The motto behind KKUMER Playground is based on a true Biblical story of Joseph, where Joseph was mocked by his brothers for his dream "Here Comes that Dreamer". It is our vision to "help making good influence in the world through business by people who dream for a better world and grow together". We are to help young generation who are struggling to make impossible possible, despaired because of unfair opportunities and trying to live their authentic dreams, a dream that makes the world better.

There are many colleagues who walk besides me in my struggles, hardships and challenges. However, it is solely my responsibility to establish a vision, organize a group and lead the business. It was the sense of mission that got me through the journey of hardship that everyone saw it was impossible. It is surely one of my strengths to overcome struggles and make the impossible possible. However it was almost impossible do well in all projects and businesses that I was involved in. It is not one man's task to manage multiple tasks such as seeking new opportunities and reading the ever changing business environment at the same time, building team work while understanding cultural emotions of the young generation and growing business and investing in people while implementing systematic strategies. It cannot be done by one person to drive the vision forward while managing multi tasks. As a matter of a fact, I cannot deny my physical restrictions as I was aging even though my heart has not changed a bit ever since the beginning. It was therefore natural thing to recognize a need to build more powerful team.

The biggest asset for the last ten years for me is not business partners, fancy business space, business reference nor accomplishments. The biggest asset and gift for me at the end of my journey is juniors who have walked towards the same dream, vision, philosophy and value together with me, whom I have watched them mature from their humble beginnings as a worker in the society to socially respectful figures who can play multiple roles per person. I have called those amongst them who have a deep understanding of KKUMER Playground's vision and global startup ecosystem who are able to draw the next vision of KKUMER Playground together. We walked close or sometime far distant to become an expert in what we do and become partners of life's journey from students to teacher relationship whom I used to encourage.

A group of students who prayed for the land of Israel and Korea's next generation together and now have become experts such as startup founders, consultants and artists. Some have become renowned data analyst, IT expert and ESG and social innovator who receive great job offers from various cooperations and organizations. There are also contents artists who create their unique contents based on their own philosophy and perspective to change the world and earnest experts in their own created field of expertise. The next ten years of KKUMER Playground is at the hands of these juniors who know the current economy, politics, technology, culture and trend better than I do and more able than I am.

My role in the next ten years is to provide time and space for KKUMER Playground for the next generation's entrepreneurs to share the vision and provide rich network and infrastructure for them to liberately extend their dreams. Instead of insisting ways of past generation's culture and business philosophy and system, transitioning the leadership to the next generation, trusting their perspectives, abilities and supporting their leadership for a better KKUMER Playground, is the ideal responsibility of senior generation. Unfortunately, authoritarian mindset is prevalent in many of today's organizations and companies where one CEO is in control of everything, indulged in the past honor and success to invade every little area of the business.

We need to support and trust the next generation who received higher level of education, experienced social changes, stayed in the fields, centering around the trends and thus are able to cater the future wiser than older generation. We as senior generation are only to cautiously advise them instead of teaching and observe and endure their shortcomings and encourage them. We are to encourage the up and coming generation instead of judging them by discovering their unique characteristics as positive assets instead of downfall. We need to abandon authoritarian attitude to teach and oppress them but our existential essence lies in patience, support, attitudes to learn and finally plant value and philosophy to direct the community for sustainable growth. It is more influential for peers to give advice who share same vision and philosophy than advice give from older generation.

I am drawing a future of KKUMER Playground to be a playground that holds a worldview of connecting young generation's cultural emotions to understanding current generation for more young people to literately play in the ground for the next ten years. However our essential value still lays in investing in young entrepreneurs, bridging Korea and Israel to contribute to Korea's startup ecology system. There is a change in means of accomplishing vision and keyword. There are many keywords that represent the fourth industrial revolution but we focus on Web 3.0 area. Those who invested in blockchain for the last ten years, an area which was seemingly impossible, are now leading the digital transformation, owning large share in this area.

In this transitioning verge of digital transformation, there are many new keywords appearing such as Coin, NFT, DAO and DiFi. The first founded company by KKUMER Playground, Future IT & Society (FITS) is a Think Tank that explores various areas of technology and trend such as startup, economy, society, education and culture and experiments various ideas and imaginations of the unknown possibilities as a result of transition from Web 2.0 to Web 3.0. FITS does its best to prepare for the future or a future that is already here with us by cooperating with cooperations, public institution, startups and founders to recommend the ideal attitudes towards the new era and build business environment infrastructure through technology collaboration and discover sustainable business. FITS suggests solution for those who are worried about the future society including founders by consulting projects and startup education and seminars.

Space business by KKUMER Playground is also changing. We extend our space business from F&B business by turning trendy and rest mood of cafe at Hapjeong-dong and restaurant at Namsan into a business community space for CEOs. F&B by KKUMER Playground is creating our own identity by hiring new leaders to pioneer in new market of Food Technology that serves experiences and values beyond fancy space and good food.

It is true that we still have many challenges ahead even after successfully launched a dream team and its dynamics to build the future of KKUMER

Playground to solve the next ten years of industry and make the next generations' dreams come true. There are many huddles awaiting to pursue the same dream by a group of people who have had different backgrounds in expertise and culture. The challenges include integration of different philosophies and cultures in segmented work areas, uniformed perception of result and speed of work, respect for each individual's expertise and style while generating actual performance and these are just some of challenges we need to resolve in order to build an ideal systematic organization.

Against all odds, we chose a difficult road once again. Because this difficult road is the only road to generate a new perspective and competence and paint the dream team's big picture through healthy conflict and debate to draw a deep understanding for each other. This painful learning process would be another laughing matter in our KKUMER Playground ten years later, a history and story that we co-wrote. I believe learning through team work is the best method to help the young generation grow, support and cooperate.

KKUMER Playground is a playground of dreamers who dream, fail and grow from these failures. It is becoming a strong community of trust and bond where team members rely on each other in difficulties instead of verbal commitment who only discuss the new future of Web 3.0, ESG, Digital Transformation and Metaverse. Conferences and work hours of KKUMER Playground could be seen as ineffective. However our team has high interest in what kind of dreams they are to draw and how to grow based on individual's vision and value in comparison to other institutions.

We think it is very important to build an environment where people can freely share their stories of life, love, marriage, raising children, achieving dreams whilst maintaining happy marriages and dreams and visions even if they seem vague. Unlike my generation, the current young generation could find it hard to share dreams, visions and ideals that often seem unrealistic. Generation MZ has a extremely realistic culture but I want to be with those who talk about their dreams and make their dreams come true.

Second - Korea's Global Startup Hub for the Next Generation
South Korea has been supporting many young entrepreneurs based on strong strategies to activate startup ecology system at a national level, which was built around small and medium-sized enterprises venture department since Park Chung-hee administration's startup economy. South Korea has had a nation wide startup boom which resulted in implementing startup support projects per institution ranging from public to private sectors. Experts and interested parties are now assessing the realistic outcomes of a decade of efforts to strategically support startups and measuring new strategies for the next road map.

South Korea has already advanced as a startup nation as many startup support systems such as education, incubation and globally renowned startup program such as TIPS have successfully been executed. small and medium-sized enterprises venture department has already announced a new plan for the next ten years to activate and advance Korea's startup ecology system and there are many news articles headlining new unicorn companies.

It is a lot of time and money consuming work for a private sector to participate in startup support ecosystem without government or large cooperation's fund and business model that secures sustainable cash flow. It is for this reason that astronomical scale of fund is implemented from public sectors and cooperations also support startups as a part of their CSR work and the trend of having an 'open innovation' department in order to connect with innovation to the company's internal departments has rapidly swooped.

Since Startup Economy Innovation Center was established ten years ago, I have endured in this industry and have realized that investing in an entrepreneur, takes a large amount of time and energy and it takes extra patience to see the outcomes.

However the ability to persistently drive in this startup industry came from the integrity engraved by mission. I have founded and maintained (Global Youth Startup, GYS) community to constantly help young entrepreneurs grow even in situations where there were people who had to take a break, I provided personal help.

From these relationships, I could carry on investing in the next generation who share and agree with the same vision and philosophy. It was the root of this encouraging relationship that has the authentic power to help the juniors to go through failures more than angel investments at the early stage.

Startups usually do not succeed at their first try. Despite of knowing this fact, I still support and invest in them. Because this experience and opportunity become the seed to bloom their potential to grow as a global entrepreneur who has strong basics based on failures and a wide perspective to understand business fields.

We are building our own system to discover entrepreneurs who have capacity and insight to help other CEOs in different industries through our expertise curriculum to incubate young CEOs in their expertise that was advanced from our initial community startup education and investment and consulting methods.

Members of KKUMER Playground are categorized by a few layers based on their role and function of those roles. First layer is young CEOs who start a startup based on their values and philosophies. Those young CEOs build virtual market and customer theory and build their team who agree with their startups' visions.

The second layer is Teammate who helps the CEOs and cooperate with them in the field. They share the burden of difficult tasks of early startups and numerous business and tasks. They are the core engine who raise and grow the startup under the same vision even though they may lack in expertise.

The third layer is Builder. Builder is a group of experts who provide support in actual administrative works for CEOs to overcome various problems that are met during the business growth and solve them.

The fourth layer is Mentor; a group of senior veteran entrepreneurs who are enriched with business experiences and understanding. They play a supporting role for startups to grown both quantity and quality wise through mentoring, distribution channels, network and infrastructure.

The fifth layer is Community Member, referring to all who are connected in various programs and projects in KKUMER Playground. It operates in a more flexible network who are preparing for open opportunities of KKUMER Playground to found a startup, help a startup or act as an expert whenever they want.

KKUMER Playground directly supports young entrepreneurs to grow through various human resource and network. Space business for young entrepreneurs is transforming into various dimensions. KKUMER Space which started off as an incubating center with independent offices for young startups has expanded its dimension as a resting place such as cafe and roof top terrace and an art gallery and community space for local residents and young entrepreneurs.

KKUMER Playground is also located at Pankyo Startup Campus called SOSA Korea and a newly launched restaurant, called The Hills Namsan, which is also expanding its functions and roles. KKUMER Playground now holds more than ten types of spacial roles such as gallery office to work in the space that exhibits artworks of some of the best Korea's artists, young business man lounge with restaurant and cafe, co-working space open for everyone and library.

All spaces run by KKUMER Playground counts young entrepreneurs as our top tier clients even though these spaces serve various roles such as work, rest, business meeting, networking, education or seminar. As long as KKUMER Playground stays inspiring for them from the harmonious relationship between entrepreneurs, residents, experts and investors endorsed by the spacial value created by KKUMER Playground, it will likely to expand constantly.

There are various demographics of different backgrounds, experiences, ages and diversity present at KKUMER Playground from startup teams who prove their thesis in business field, those in charge of education and consulting to help startups and branding and marketing creatives to suggest brand philosophy. Because of these diverse areas of expertise, another important area is collaboration. NFT project founded by Web 3.0 study group that belong to Future IT & Society (FITS) is progressively at work.

To lead this project, four core leaders constitute TF. One member is experienced and highly skilled in ESG and social impact who has a background as a social venture startup founder. Second member is in charge of trends, technology and providing actionable network and human resource of Web 3.0, who has a background as an IT/Tech consultant. Third member is in charge of art & creative area including videos, contents, branding, marketing and merchandise development such as characters and goods. The last member plays a RA role who has a background in managing female entrepreneur community. The team constitutes of ideal members according to their characteristics and capacity.

KKUMER Playground defines collaboration as a project team of members who have different backgrounds and expertise that form TF type group in order to achieve short and long term goals to demonstrate thesis at a pre-stage of a startup. A group discussion becomes contents and stories told by each individual becomes a strategy. This group of talented people who already have adequate experiences and professionalism in their expertise taking the challenge based on a new thesis is a type of 'play' that KKUMER Playground is talking about and the best contents.

The three functions and areas that KKUMER Playground is promoting as an organization is to provide a platform for dreamers, a community that supports and helps them grow and a company builder for struggling startups to rely and grow together. Many opportunities are provided to those who are connected in KKUMER Playground; young entrepreneurs, senior entrepreneurs, investors and experts in different areas, through various community programs that people can communicate in. The programs include weekly worship meeting in Namsan called D.WIN (Dreamer's Worship in Namsan), network that has supported cooperation and networking for senior entrepreneurs, CEO MBA and a program that invests in and educates young entrepreneurs, Next CEO Community.

Our communities are more than a business platform but a vision platform that shares the same vision, that is to support up and coming entrepreneurs.

We are also a strong community that shares difficulties of running businesses and burdens of life. The core members of KKUMER Playground all have the same passion, that is to support the next generation and young entrepreneurs. Although these core members are still young and have not accomplished big success in certain expertise like senior entrepreneurs yet they are already generous enough to devout their lives for the next generation.

These devout young leaders of KKUMER Playground truly know what is more valuable in life than fortune and fame. Because of this great companionship with fellow workers, KKUMER Playground could have been directed into a healthy community. The last function of the community is Company Builder, which we make our own ways.

The Company Builder model is generally preferred by cooperations and investment companies with a large fund. Although we are not as financially able as established financial entities, KKUMER Playground has our own philosophy that the essence of a successful startup lies in a person rather than investment fund. When providing experimental field to test entrepreneurs' business thesis, unafraid of failures, to acknowledge individual's vision and to expand their dreams liberally, it shapes the best team. Shortage of financial status can easily be solved through KKUMER Playground's partnership network that connects influential investors and financiers.

Our biggest strength is the ability to discover startups of solid capacity and clear vision based on trust and our unique culture and system to enable sustainable growth of startups. This is our unique approach and theory towards Company Builder model.

Third - Contribution to Korea's Global Startup Ecosystem

Israel is world's renowned nation for world's most advanced technologies and an advanced startup nation who endlessly discovers of new startups that innovate of technology inventions through Israel's startup ecosystem instead of allowing monopoly by certain cooperations. There are many aspects to Israel's fame as a startup nation including Israel's customs, history, culture, outstanding DNA, geological restrictions of being surrounded by enemy countries and their strong drive on growth strategy through becoming a technology centered country.

Israel is a country that foresaw the great potential in global market entry for economic growth long time ago with united efforts pursued by government, universities and many other society's influential institutions with significant roles. There is a saying in Israel; "There are people who have not tried startup yet but there is no one who wouldn't try a startup once in their life time in Israel", which indicates that the popular norm of founding a startup across all ages from a youngster to a senior citizen as a means to survival and growth. Especially, a nation with a limited internal market smaller than South Korea will always target global market for their startups. How has Israel built the exclusive culture to normalize global startup?

First of all, it is due to Israel's global startup network stretching from Tel Aviv to Silicon Valley involving cooperations, institutions and persons.

Although Tel Aviv is not widely known in South Korea comparatively, Tel Aviv is an original global city that directly shares core technologies and human resources worldwide and it is a tabloid edition for Silicon Valley. Tel Aviv is a city that resembles its appearance to USA with small details like vehicle's number plate.

Israel considers their native business culture as identical to Silicon Valley's and a natural process to enter global market. It can be easily demonstrated in NASDAQ's listed companies how close Israel and Silicon Valley's fund is linked together and work in the same context. The top countries that has the highest expenditure on R&D per GDP are Israel ranked as number one, followed by South Korea ranked as number two.

However Israel has already taken over global market in all areas of industry with high market share, however why is South Korea still unable to overcome the huddle of global startup?

South Korea needs to target global market through strategical projects founded by prominent youngsters it their process of building a startup. South Korea has a vague fear about global market for our nation is one of few countries that has lived a long history as a single ethnicity, which contributed to Korea's closed economic system.

Despite of Korea's closed economy system, Korea is a strong startup nation that has a great potential. If South Korea can overcome language barrier and unexplainable fear of global market, it is highly possible to launch many innovative startups. KKUMER Playground is a place to adopt Israel's DNA of global entrepreneurship based on the network with Israeli VIPs. It is still a remarkable accomplishment of Korea's startup ecosystem to bear many VCs who boosted growth of startups at early stage. However there is still an absence of VCs who can embed a perspective and attitude for global market for Korean startups.

On the other hand, KKUMER Playground consistently discusses global entrepreneurship through our exclusive education and workshop curriculum embracing all critical startup stages from making business model and projects targeting global market to connecting to global investment when startups generate quantity and quality outcomes to help them penetrate into global market based on our excellent network of Israeli VIPs.

Furthermore, KKUMER Playground is built on the structural startup ecosystem that connects Korea's entrepreneurs for field inspection to experience Israel's unique startup culture and ecosystem that further leads to investment assessment by Israel-based global VCs. There has not been any case for Korea's startup to have received investment from Israeli VC for Korea is still behind in terms of technology advancement, however I am very positive that we are not too far away from bearing the first star startup for the recognition of Israel's global VCs in three years of time.

Another critical downside that need to be addressed about Korea startups is how Korea's Confucian culture that emphasizes politeness and etiquette between people is considered relevant culture in business world. The influence of Confucian culture can be found in Korea's dialectic language that has a tendency to use variant adjectives and honorific titles to show respect and care for others.

However in business world where it values core value and efficiency, Confucian culture is still prominently present in Korea's business narrative. A good example of it would be many early workers in society in Korea find it challenging to write business emails. Koreans are expected to speak in polite forms and greetings especially when the recipient is an elderly or holds higher position.

One might consider the culture a positive thing however when manners and formality are accumulated, it often results in a major inefficiency. Short and precise communication of English culture eliminates all necessary messages with minimum formality. The importance of process efficiency is regarded critical in administrative area.

In Korea, the administrative process for government related startup projects is unnecessarily complicated as it involves government fund that requires fulfilling multiple pages of documents such as business plan. It is almost like learning new language and culture of a foreign land. The longevity and complicatedness of government led process of startup project can be expected qualities as public institutions count fairness and publicity very important. However it is paralyzing process for startups who have to operate at high speed and efficiency.

How about formality protocol culture for high social hierarchy figures? It is true that many of authoritarian and formal layers have been removed, but still unnecessary formality remains in Korea's business culture. One cannot deny that those are beautiful cultural heritage of Korea's history but it is also undeniable that it creates unnecessary inefficiencies in business world.

For example, Yossi Vardi attended the third Korea and Israel Business Forum as a main speaker. One of prominent entrepreneurs of Korea voluntarily offered to escort Yossi Vardiafter his speech finished. When he was trying to escort him to the parking lot, Yossi Vardi responded questioning "Why are you walking me to the parking lot when I know where my car is?"

I am not saying all cultures of Israel or Western English speaking countries are more superior than Korea's. Maintaining Korea's heritage and culture are important but we need to renew our cultural minds when doing business in global startup ecosystem.

If I am not mistaken, I am proud to say that I am one of few people who understand Israel's business culture and language based on my ten year experience in networking with top Israeli VIPs in their finance and political realm. Unexpected connection with Prime Minister Olmert has led to reach unimaginable relationships with other influential figures of Israel and after years of efforts put into Korea and Israel relation has proved my genuine heart for Israel to bring us close to become business partners who can openly discuss anything anytime.

Early years of the work focused on holding business forums between two countries in order to provide networking stage for representatives of both countries including entrepreneurs, politicians and education leaders and these business forums have helped to raise awareness of Korean influence in Israel's startup ecosystem. Most impressive accomplishment from Korea and Israel Business Forum is launching Korean branch of global accelerator, SOSA, which accelerated data-based innovation hub as a result of advanced cooperation through business trips, open innovation projects, endorsed by the city of New York.

Finally, the time has come for full committed relation between Korea and Israel based on trust built for a long time. The foundation for globalization of Korea's startup ecosystem through intimate networking between young startups and VCs also between major institutions of both countries has been laid. Our goals are to found an institution like Israel Innovation Authority for discovering new future industries for Korea and developing strategies for it also to lay a foundation of army startup ecosystem which enables national technology talents to develop technologies and prepare startups during their military service and finally establishing startup ecosystem in Pankyo in order to prove Pankyo as Korea's Silicon Valley in the global scene.

Of all definitions of startup, one of the most famous definitions would be a definition introduced in the book Lean Startup by Eric Riise, who defines a startup as "an individual or a team who continuously invent and validate a thesis in order to introduce innovative product and service that did not exist before". Even though KKUMER Playground grows in size and experiences, our essence stays as a startup. A startup that is not afraid of challenges and experiments for new innovations therefore we continue to dream and write a new story.

An organization that restricts itself in conventional system of rich resources, complicated decision making structure and pressure of always having to accomplish something, will always consider Israel and global market entry as unnecessarily too difficult of a task. However it is possible for KKUMER Playground because we are a startup. It is the upmost important bucket list of KKUMER Playground to embed global DNA in Korea's startup ecosystem despite of whom our partners are and what our methods are, based on meaningful experiences and capacities we have built from failures.

CHAPTER 04

Technologies that Change the World

Self Driving Car is the Key to Future

What would be Korea's future industry be? I am a person who lived at the verge of the last generation of Korea's industrialization. When I was a college student, democracy bloomed in Korea's society. When I was in middle school, there was democratization uprising starting in Gwangju and it met its peak when I was a college student. Many colleagues of mine fought in the democratization uprising and many of them have become politicians. I have experienced both industrialization and democratization and seen the realities of these two ideology. I am from the generation that was positioned in between the two significant historic

▲ Mobileye, Israel's leading AI computer vision startup sold to Intel for 17.56 trillion KRW.

events of South Korea.

Now I have become a middle aged man in no time. I have become one of Korea's social leadership in my mid fifties. I went to study overboard in USA in my twenties, experienced global business world, became friends with global Jewish entrepreneurs and learned how Israel has achieved global entrepreneurship and a global leading country. When Israelis found a startup, they build English website foremost instead of their native language Hebrew, to target global market.

The reason behind excellent leadership behind Israel's world's economy influence for thousand years is due to their outstanding insight to foresee the future and that enabled them to prepare and manage the future. For example, when Israelis traders made a lot of money, robbers watched for opportunities to steal their cash. So they sought after ways to safely secure their cash, which led to an invention of credit card. It is also Israelis who found a global banking system to activate credit card use worldwide.

These Israelites then made the central bank finance policies, which dominate world's finance, into a blockchain money. Israelites are interested in profitable business and innovations to demolish any ineffective old systems and regulations for a future society rather than short-term advantageous goals of Israel as a nation or corporations. In order for Korea to survive in the global competence, we have to build intimate relationship with Israel to prepare for radical changes in soon coming future.

▲ Tri-Eye, Israel's best startup with night vision AI technology.

One of recent projects that Israelites are after is 'auto-mobility'. Auto-mobility will make radical shift in all aspects of our society in the near future. We have already experienced express trains and their impacts in our everyday life. From Seoul to Busan, it used to take five hours by cars but express trains shortened the duration to be only two hours and it made a huge impact in our society.

Auto-mobility will make a huge impact in our society. Firstly, it will eventually redeem drivers from horrendous hours of driving. Interior design for seatings in the car will change into a circular design, which will turn the car space into a little office. Many business meetings will be held in cars and new business opportunities will be generated to give new purposes to this newly invented space and time in auto-mobile vehicles.

Auto-mobile vehicles will also resolve air pollution, which is one of the most serious issues in the world. Rechargeable electric cars will reduce the amount of CO2 emission and help to slow global warming. It is also expected to reduce many car accidents, which are mostly occurred by drivers for 94% of the time. It is also the only way to reduce traffic jam.

If we think about all vehicles driving in and out of Seoul and Gyeonggi-do including buses and cars, these vehicles cause intense traffic jam and air pollution everyday. However new plan with the introduction of automobile vehicles is that there will be an enormous parking lot at the entrance of the district Seoul and auto-mobile buses and cars will take the ride for passengers from there. There will be many auto-mobile stops and stations all throughout the city.

Auto-mobile vehicles will not only apply to vehicles on the road but it can also drive private helicopters to deliver passengers all around Seoul. The future that auto-mobile vehicles will bring is beyond our imagination. However, we talk about auto-mobile vehicles like it's a fictional story and we are missing out many business opportunities.

It's not too late. I strongly believe the key to future society's change is auto-mobile vehicles. We will be left out in the global competence if we do not prepare for auto-mobile vehicle related businesses. The core capacity behind auto-mobile vehicle industry is IT technology. This is the reason why we need to grow strong IT startups specializing in cyber security, navigation, smart mobility, artificial eye and smart vehicle sensor program.

I am already seeing auto-mobile vehicle industry that Israel is preparing for. There are about 100 auto-mobile vehicles by MobilEye driving on the streets of Jerusalem city. However Korea does not even have regulations set for auto-mobile vehicles. There is an infamous episode in regards to self-driving cars in Korea. Korea's government suspended a founder of self-driving car startup as he was driving and he had to move his startup to America.

I am already seeing auto-mobile vehicle industry that Israel is preparing for. There are about 100 auto-mobile vehicles by MobilEye driving on the streets of Jerusalem city. However Korea does not even have regulations set for auto-mobile vehicles. There is an infamous episode in regards to self-driving cars in Korea. Korea's government suspended a founder of self-driving car startup as he was driving and he had to move his startup to America.

How should we prepare the future? Where would Korea's place be in the future? I hope those who make decisions on nations's policies and visions to have an insight to read the future. I beg of Korea government to remove all business restrictions in regards to auto- mobile vehicles. Korea as a nation needs to pour all our ability and power into auto-mobile vehicle regulations and finance. Of little help as I am, I would like to contribute for the future generation and future of our nation.

Self Driving Car is the Major Future Industry of Korea

Self-driving car is not only about driving without a driver. Yes, it does provide that convenience but there is a larger technology behind it. It is an implication of all advanced IT technologies including artificial intelligence, sensor, security, simulation and smart city. Only nations and societies who prepare the future based on collaboration of these cutting edge technologies can survive. I learned something very important in my business trip to Israel about self driving car technology.

If one does not prepare for the future, he will fall behind. Only those

▲ Israeli self-driving car simulation company Cognata.

whose purpose is innovation rather than their own nation or society's benefits are capable of preparing for the future. One has to go nuts.

A pioneer has to do something to prepare a promising future industry. If one relies one's life on government policies or institutional systems, I think he is hugely mistaken.

Moreover, when I was in Israel, there was an incident where Korean police prosecuted 'TADA'. In this nonsensical situation, I could do nothing but broke into a vain laughter. When I encounter some people who prepare future too comfortably, I could not help but wonder how our nation would make a living in the future. Koreans are living in a generation more difficult than the late period of Joseon dynasty. Are we to live for the future or just settle in the comfort zone?

Republic of Korea has globally renowned technologies. We are a miraculous nation that has become world's economic power based on strong manufacturing industry. When Sony in Japan fell behind Samsung in Korea, the game was over between Korea and Japan. Korea's manufacturing business has world's top technology and research power in semiconductor, ship, vehicles and etc. Many countries are marbled by Korea's success over such a short period of time. However, Korea's economic strength in manufacturing business is threatened by vigorous chaser, China and China will soon take over Korea's place.

Then what would be the solution? I personally do not believe that the miracle of Han-river will last long. Because the world is simply changing too fast. How can we chase such a shift change? We can only learn it from Israel. Especially, self-driving car industry can bring the second Han-river miracle.

Unfortunately, the biggest huddle for the self-driving technology is Korea's legal restrictions.
How do governments in Israel and USA help to foster self-driving car business? In Israel, the government voluntarily built roads for self-driving cars. In USA, they signed legal exemptions for self-driving cars. In China, they opened all self-driving car development technologies before any law enforcement.

Korea needs to eliminate restrictions. We are to implement necessary technologies for the future first even it sparks some social controversies. 'SNOW', Korea's startup for self- driving cars had to stop their test and immigrate to USA due to the legal restrictions in Korea. Even though Korea's government encourages entrepreneurs to innovate IT technologies, they do not have a strong will to lift related legal restrictions.

Self-driving car is the biggest business sector in the future industry. This is an inevitable demand of our future generation. However only Korea is falling behind in this competition. We need to lift all legal restrictions when developing IT technologies for newly emerging industries. If we delay in responding needs of self-driving car industry in any accountable actions because of legal restrictions, we will become underdeveloped country like Venezuela. We need a political figure of leader to bravely action for a radical innovation. I am hoping for these figures to rise soon.

Cyber Security
is the Core Technology of Self Driving Car

The major future industry of Israel is self-driving car. The core strength of smart mobility lays in those who first invented cutting edge technologies and successfully commercialized them. Since 2013, Israel gave a 100% for developing smart mobility by investing in pioneering startups. It was a strategic collaboration between government and civil cooperations to come up with policy support and financial investment. Their investment in future industry of smart mobility was successful. After only five years, the investment has achieved underlying accomplishments.

▲ Israeli self-driving car global security company Argus Vice President's PT.

In smart mobility, there has to be collaborated efforts from various technologies. Artificial eye for human eye, virtual driving software program and engineering for checking conditions of auto driving, a special camera with infrared light sensor to gain a clear sight in the night, security to protect and prevent outside hacking attempts to cause many dangers to car drivers such as car accidents and many more technologies have to collaborate in order to execute successful smart mobility.

One of pioneering companies in smart mobility that I want to write about is 'Argus'. Tel Aviv based company, Argus was a smart mobility security specialized startup founded by three developers in 2013. Their goal is to protect smart mobility by supplying extensive network security solution to prevent any possible crimes. They developed exclusive quality cybersecurity solution for self driving cars to secure safety of a vehicle both inside and out.

The most cautious aspect of smart mobility and its commercialization is the protection against outside hackings. Without hacking prevention, program operated smart mobility is exposed to outside dangers such as terror. 'Argus' developed cyber security of smart mobility with electric control device, tele matrix device, infotainment center and operation under advanced operation system of Linux, Android, Adative AUTOSAR in connection with ADAS device.

Moreover, their inside vehicle network security assesses vehicle's total network communication and stops internal crash of the vehicle and virus attack. Protection by core electric control device such as dashboard,

BCM(Body Control Module) control system, gateway, makes the vehicle's operation seamless. Argus has a firm cyber security philosophy for smart mobility and it now has its offices around the world in Michigan, Silicon Valley, Stuttgart and Tokyo with its headquarter in Tel Aviv.

What is a secret behind for such a remarkable growth for a startup to grow into one of world's top smart mobility cyber security company in just six years? Because they developed exclusive smart mobility technologies based on their cyber security background. All three founders of Argus are all engineer technicians. Also, Argus would not have existed without Israel army Unit 8200 as 60% of all employees of Argus are from Unit 8200, which is the best intelligent army in Israel.

A team full of Unit 8200 army of Argus succeeded in 50 hacking projects with 100% success rate. One of recent hacking projects was to ascertain whether a vehicle was hacked or not by hacking tens of trailers via smartphone while figuring out whether the hacking was controlled or not. Argus team has successfully resolved the task and is currently developing and testing various algorithms and vaccine programs to fight various hacking programs.

Israel is actively preparing for future industry. It is the insight to read the next generation's industry that can make the next generation happy and prosperous. In Korea, there is a decline of many of our prosperous industries such as 'ship, steel, semi-conductor, architecture' that once made Korea a wealthy nation. If we do not change economic
structure that relies too much on conglomerates, we are likely to fall into

underdeveloped countries like South American countries like Argentina and Chile. How shall we construct the future?

We need to question. We are to inform the next generation that the world is swiftly changing. We have to come out of our economic comfort zone that was once secured by legends of ship, steel and semi-conductor industries which keeps us missing out opportunities for future industry. We are to invest in startups who have exclusive technologies to grow into a global leader. This is time to discover small yet powerful companies to transform them as a globally advancing startup. And it is cyber security of smart mobility that I am focusing on.

Metaverse;
Worldview and Storytelling beyond Technology

The hottest content is Metaverse in Korea. It feels like you are behind the trend if you don't know what Metaverse is. We are constantly exposed to a society flooded with new information. Thousands and thousands of new pieces of information enter our brain through the internet. One of IT contents that is trending now is Metaverse. How should we interpret the future's Metaverse business?

When we mention IT business, most people link the idea to technology and distribution channel. Of course, for IT contents to be consumed, it needs implementation of various IT technologies such as big data, IoT, cyber security, blockchain and etc. However these cutting edge technologies are not what IT business is all about. Likewise, when we discuss Metaverse, these technologies are necessary methods for Metaverse but they are not the fundamental essence of Metaverse.

Let's imagine that high end fashion label, Gucci created Metaverse world. Many people would wonder why. Because Gucci is a fashion brand, not an IT company. This could leave many people curious as it is quite hard to grasp the crossover between these two seemingly disparate topics. However, Gucci has already made a clever use of IT technology using Metaverse to their fashion empire and is creating enormous value and culture beyond

▲ Gucci Metaverse Platform

our imagination. This is the powerful insight of global fashion label, Gucci. Metaverse platform by Gucci allows users to purchase luxury Gucci items at affordable price for avatars for only $3 online. Why does Gucci invest in Metaverse? It is because Gucci invented new online value for their luxury goods in online stores rather than offline. This inspiration does not come from IT technologies but by worldview and story telling executed via IT technologies to create new online profits. Likewise, the key to Metavese success lays in one's ability to unravel worldview and storytelling rather than IT technology itself.

The most important tactics for successful business are value and philosophy. Quality products or cutting edge technologies do not always lead to good sales. Number one technology is not made by distribution channels. The number one company with market capitalization is Apple. Is Apple better than Samsung in terms of technology advancement? No. If we only look at technology advancement, Apple is actually behind Samsung. However Apple is the number one company in smartphone.

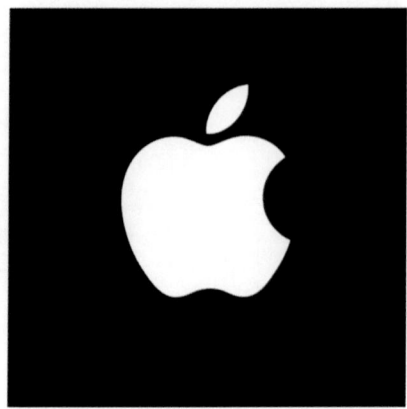

▲ Apple logo.

What is the reason behind this?

Apple's smartphone reflects their value and philosophy. This is why Samsung cannot overthrow Apple even it has more advanced technologies than Apple. Many Apple maniacs fall for Apple's design and philosophy and they hardly switch to Samsung's products. Why do so many Apple fans not change their smartphone brand preference? Apple is brilliant at telling their brand philosophy as a story. Apple's ability to link their value and philosophy to business by optimizing their story telling, is exquisite.

The same mechanism applies to Metaverse. Metavese technologies cannot last long without worldview and storytelling. One can always employ technicians with adequate wage. However, IT technicians do not have ability to create a creative worldview and story telling. This is why creative minds in liberal arts need to collaborate with logical minds in natural science first.

Especially for contents makers of Metaverse, it is crucial to have an insight for paradigm shifts of the world and generational turn overs.

In Metaverse, outer appearances such as age, gender, degrees are not important. It is only avatars that play in virtual reality that matter. There are no regulations and rules but only fun and reason of existence for their avatars. Therefore, it is value and technology behind Metaverse that matter instead of technologies that built Metaverse. The key to success in Metaverse is to discover story tellers who can create world views based on humanity qualities.

▲ The world of various metaverses.

There was a Metaverse alliance formed between government, companies, schools and hospitals in May at Pankyo. Korea is building virtual reality of Metaverse and trying new businesses. As mentioned earlier, the success of Metaverse business relies on story telling instead of IT technologies. I see a future where a generation aged between 10-20 hang out at Metaverse. I hope many creative story tellers in Korea to lead global Metaverse realm.